A Straightforward Guide to

THE PLANNING SYSTEM AND PLANNING PERMISSIONS IN THE UK.

Roger Sproston BA, MSc

Straightforward Publishing
www.straightforwardbooks.co.uk

Straightforward Guides

© Roger Sproston 2024

All rights reserved. No part of this publication may be reproduced in a retrieval system or transmitted by any means, electronic or mechanical, photocopying or otherwise, without the prior permission of the copyright holders.

978-1-80236-350-0

Printed by 4edge www.4edge.co.uk

Cover design by BW Studio Derby

Whilst every effort has been made to ensure that the information contained within this book is correct at the time of going to press, the author and publisher can take no responsibility for the errors or omissions contained within.

Contents

Introduction

Part 1. Understanding the current planning system -a general overview.   15

An overview of the planning system in the UK	15
Green Belt reform	16
Preserving the purposes of the Green Belt	17
National Development Management Policies (NDMPs)	17
Golden rules for development	18
Where is planning policy set out?	18
How are planning applications decided?	20
The role of views of local residents	21
Deciding a planning application	21
Can planning permission be overturned?	22
Judicial review	22
Enforcing planning breaches	23
Role of the Local Government Ombudsman	24
Levelling-up and Regeneration Act 2023	24
Planning differences in Scotland Wales and Northern Ireland	30
Scotland	30
Wales	31
Northern Ireland	31
Common Themes	32

Part 2. Planning Use Classes — 35

Planning Use Classes — 35

Permitted development-change from commercial to residential — 42

Certificate of Lawful Use — 42

Proposed changes to planning use for intended Airbnb use — 43

Part 3. Obtaining planning permission — 45

The process of applying for planning permission — 47

Types of planning application — 47

Non-planning consents — 48

Application for full planning permission — 48

Outline planning application — 49

What are reserved matters? — 49

Which authority should deal with a planning application? — 51

Land in more than one local planning authority area — 51

Development to be undertaken by a local authority — 52

Development to be undertaken by the Crown — 53

Requirements to make a valid application — 54

Where can the standard application form be found? — 54

Making a planning application on paper — 55

Copies of the application form — 55

The Community Infrastructure Levy — 56

National information requirements — 56

Plans and drawings — 57

What information should be included on a location plan? — 60

Ownership Certificate and Agricultural Land Declaration	60
Making a planning application for someone else's land	62
What is an agricultural land declaration?	63
Design and Access Statement	63
Application for listed building consent	66
Outline planning applications details	67
Reserved matters with an outline application	68
Environmental Impact Assessment	69
Local information requirements	69
Changes to the description of development	70
Local planning authority has served a non-validation notice	73
Application for a development already refused	74
Changes after validation of an application	75
Appealing against a planning decision	76
Costs of applying for planning permission	81
Part 4. Building regulations and the role of Building Inspectors.	**85**
Building regulations as of 2024	85
Building Control Process for Higher-Risk Buildings:	86
Wider Changes to Procedural Building Regulations:	87
Permitted Development Rights:	87
Do I need building regulations approval?	90
Building regulations application fee	94

Different types of building regulation applications	94
Building notice application for building regs	95
The inspection process for building regs	99
How do I get a completion certificate?	99
Selling a house without building regs	100
What is the competent person scheme?	101

Part 5. Party Wall Agreements explained	**103**
The Party Wall Act 1996	103
Party Wall defined	104
Walls that are not Party Walls:	105
When do I need a Party Wall Agreement?	105
Is it a legal requirement to have a Party Wall Agreement?	106
Can you create a Party Wall Agreement yourself?	107
Nature of the agreement	108
Cost of a party wall agreement	108
Is a Party Wall Notice mandatory?	109
Neighbour objections	110
Assigning a Party Wall Surveyor	111
What if There is Still a Dispute?	112

Part 6. When is Planning Permission not needed?	**115**
Permitted Development Rights.	
Homeowners and Permitted Development Rights	115
What can I build or extend under permitted development?	116

What can't be built under Permitted Development?	117
Restrictions with Permitted Development	117
Prior approval	118
The Neighbourhood Consultation Scheme	119
Lawful Development Certificates	119
Permitted development categories	120
Neighbour objections	122
Construction not complying with Permitted Development	123
Planning permission for a home improvement project	123
Extensions	124
Internal walls	125
Replacing windows	126
Converting a garage	127
Rooflights	127
Loft Conversion	127
Two Storey Extensions	128
New conservatory	128
Sheds, garden office or outbuildings	129
Converting two homes into one	129
Adding another storey	130
Planning permission for a new porch	130
Adding a fence or wall	131
New garden decking	131
Swimming pools	131
Creating a new driveway	132
Creating parking spaces	132

Changing cladding	133
Solar panels to a roof	133
Basements requiring planning permission	133
Conversion of industrial/commercial buildings	134
Car charging ports	134
Outdoor security or lighting	134
Installing a Ground Source Heat Pump	135
Installing an air source heat pump	135
Work on Drains	136

Part 7. Contesting proposed developments.   **137**

Finding Out about Planned Developments	137
Making a Planning Objection to the council	138
Grounds for disputing a planning application	139
What a council will not accept as grounds for an objection	140

Part 8. Farms-Farms-Planning permission and Permitted Development Rights for Farms   **143**

When you need Planning permission	143
When you do not need it	143
Permitted development	144
What types of agricultural PDRs are there?	145
Class A	145
Class O	147
Class Q	147

Class R	148
Class S	148
Glossary of terms	151
Useful information and websites	165

Index

Appendix 1. Case study plus drawings and final planning permission for a new build house (self-build).

****

Introduction

As the title suggests, this book, written in **2024**, is, in the main, intended for the non-professional person. This might be a person who wishes to alter, in some way, their existing residence, or even to build a new home.

There may be concerns with proposed developments in the vicinity of a person's home-whether it be large-scale developments or a neighbour proposing an extension which might intrude on a neighbouring property.

In many cases, people are uncertain what to do and can feel powerless, particularly when faced with the financial and political muscle of large developers.

What this book sets out to do is to steer people through the various processes involved in planning and development and to clearly point out rights and obligations. It has avoided being overly technical and littered with arcane language, but instead is clear and concise.

Although the book is a practical introduction, aimed at helping individuals and business to solve issue they may have with planning, the first part of the book lays the foundations for an understanding of the planning system as a whole.

The book covers the following areas in detail:

- Part 1 presents an overview of the planning system in the UK.
- Part 2. Explains the meaning of Planning use Classes and their importance to understanding the planning system.
- Part 3 Works through the process of obtaining planning permission and what to do if this is not granted.
- Part 4. Explains building regulations and the role of building inspectors when carrying out works.
- Part 5. Explains the meaning and importance of Party Wall Agreements.
- Part 6. Explains to what extent people can carry out works without obtaining planning permission.
- Part 7. Explains how people can contest proposed developments in their area.
- Part 8. This part deals with farms and the elements of the planning system specific to the agricultural sector.

In appendix 1 we present a brief case study outlining the progress through design and planning of two self-builders. This should serve to put the process in context.

In summary, each of the above areas are complex, particularly contesting developments. It is hoped this brief but

Introduction

concise book will help raise awareness of the planning system in the UK (primarily England but with reference to Wales, Scotland and Northern Ireland) and equip people with an understanding of how it operates.

****

Part 1

Understanding the Current Planning System-a General Overview

> *In Part 1, we will look at the planning system as a whole, how it operates and current legislation. There is a lot to take in but many of the areas touched upon will be fleshed out on further sections. The approach here is to paint a wider picture of what and why the planning system is.*

An overview of the planning system in the UK

Recently, there have been several changes to the UK planning system, notably The Levelling-up and Regeneration Act 2023, which affects certain aspects of how planning works in this country.

We will discuss these changes further on in this chapter. In addition, at the time of writing the Labour Government has introduced the following proposed changes to the planning system, (outlined below) principally to facilitate housebuilding. This is in order to rectify the complete mess that has arisen, in terms of chronic lack of supply and exorbitant house prices and average rents.

Green Belt reform

Preserving the purposes of the Green Belt

As part of Labour's planning reforms, one significant focus is on the Green Belt. Labour pledges to protect England's Green Belt, which has remained largely unaltered since its introduction in 1955. Essentially, the Green Belt policy was specifically designed to limit the sprawl of cities.

However, Labour's latest Green Belt reform plans aim to tackle the UK's housing crisis by strategically releasing the newly termed *grey belt land* for development under specific conditions. Grey belt land is land within green belt zones that could be built upon, such as old garage sites and so on. This initiative is part of Labour's broader pledge to build 1.5 million homes over the next five years, demonstrating their commitment to addressing the nation's housing needs.

Rezoning previously used or marginal sites

Labours plan identifies over 11,000 potential grey belt sites, which could deliver around 100,000 to 200,000 new homes. This approach aims to support sustainable development while addressing the UK's housing crisis by using Green Belt land that contributes little to the Green Belt's intended purpose.

*

National Development Management Policies (NDMPs)

Labour will introduce NDMPs specifically for the Green Belt to streamline development processes and ensure consistency in policy application. What's critical here is that the revised approach includes stringent criteria to ensure that development on released Green Belt land provides significant community benefits, such as affordable housing and enhanced local amenities, while preserving areas of high environmental value. Labour will leverage existing planning powers to implement changes swiftly, avoiding the delays associated with passing new legislation.

Golden rules for development

To complement the NDMPs, Labour has proposed a set of 'golden rules' to ensure that any development on released Green Belt land benefits both communities and nature.

These rules include:
- **Affordable housing:** A minimum of 50% of the homes built on grey belt land must be affordable.
- **Public services and infrastructure:** Developments must include new public services and infrastructure such as schools, nurseries, and health centres.

- **Environmental enhancement:** Projects must contribute to local biodiversity, green spaces, and overall environmental quality.
- **Green space improvement**: Projects must include improvements to existing green spaces and avoid building on nature-rich areas.
- **Sustainable practices:** All developments must adhere to sustainable building practices and aim for low carbon footprints.

Strategic reviews

Labour says it will commit to conducting comprehensive reviews across England to identify areas within the Green Belt that could be better utilised for development. These reviews will focus on enhancing land use efficiency and meeting housing demands without compromising the Green Belt's overall integrity.

The operation of the Planning System

Where is planning policy set out?

In England, the planning system is "plan-led". What this means is that what can be built and where it is built is set out in plans, as below:

- **Local plans** are prepared by Local Planning Authorities. They set out the framework for the future development and land use in their area. A local plan identifies what development is needed, where it should go, and what land is protected.
- Then there are **Neighbourhood plans** that are prepared by parish or town councils or local groups (called neighbourhood forums). A neighbourhood plan allows a local community to shape what new buildings in its area should look like and what infrastructure should be provided.

Government planning policies are set out in the National Planning Policy Framework (NPPF) and also the accompanying Planning Practice Guidance.

Local and neighbourhood plans should be prepared in line with the National Planning Policy Framework.

Some areas with elected mayors/combined authorities, for example Greater London and the Liverpool City Region, also have a spatial development strategy that guides development for LPAs in their area.

(for differences in Wales, Scotland and Northern Ireland see further on)

How are planning applications decided?

In Part 3, we discuss in depth the steps in making a planning application and the parties involved. Below is a brief overview of the processes involved.

Most types of development require planning permission from the Local Planning authority to go ahead, although some forms of permitted development (for example, certain home improvement projects such as loft extensions and extensions generally) are exempt from that requirement. See Part 6 for more details.

A Local Planning Authority will decide a planning application in line with relevant policies in its local plan (and the neighbourhood plan, if there is one) unless "material considerations" indicate otherwise. There is no set list of material considerations, although one important material consideration is the government's National Policy Planning Framework.

Whether a particular consideration is material to a planning application will depend on the circumstances of the case. It is for the Local Planning Authority to decide in the first instance and the courts in case of a dispute. It is important to note that the courts have generally ruled that private interests such as property values in an area are not material considerations.

The role of views of local residents

Before making a planning decision, a Local Planning Authority is required to hold a public consultation to allow local residents to express their views on the proposed development. By law, the LPA is bound to take in the views of local residents when making its decision.

However, it is important to note that an LPA will not necessarily refuse planning permission if residents object to a planning application. An LPA may still grant consent if material considerations indicate otherwise.

Deciding a planning application

Most planning applications are decided by local authority planning officers. Only around 10% of applications are decided by councillors on a planning committee. These are usually applications for major developments and controversial projects. Where they exist, parish and town councils can request to be notified of planning applications to comment on them; but they are not responsible for making decisions. If an LPA refuses planning permission, applicants can appeal the decision. Most appeals are decided by an inspector working for the Planning Inspectorate, an executive agency of the Department for Levelling Up, Housing and Communities.

In rare cases, the Secretary of State can "call in" a planning application for their own determination. This is only possible up until the point at which the LPA has formally issued its decision.

Can planning permission be overturned?

There is no third-party right of appeal in planning law. This means that neighbours or other third parties who objected to an application and are upset about an LPA's decision do not have a right to appeal that decision with the Planning Inspectorate. It is also not possible to ask the Secretary of State to "call-in" a planning application once the LPA has formally issued its decision. The Secretary of State cannot use their "call-in" powers to overturn decisions made by LPAs.

Judicial review

The planning decisions of LPAs (and planning inspectors) can be challenged in court by judicial review. The court can only rule on the way in which a decision was made, not on the planning merits of the case itself. There is a strict six-week limit for applying for judicial review. To proceed, a claim for judicial review requires permission from the court. It will decide whether a claimant has a "sufficient interest" and whether the grounds for judicial review are met. If a decision is cancelled, the LPA (or planning inspector) will remake their decision, correcting any procedural mistakes identified by the court. They may reach the same decision again, for different or expanded reasons, or make a different decision.

Enforcing planning breaches

Failure to obtain planning permission where it is required or to adhere to conditions attached to planning permission constitutes a "planning breach". LPAs have a range of enforcement powers they can use to respond to planning breaches. For example, an LPA can use an enforcement notice to require a developer to remedy a planning breach; this might involve stopping works or removing a building from land.

Failure to comply with an enforcement notice is a criminal offence that can result in a fine.

Suspected planning breaches can be reported to the planning enforcement team of the LPA. It is up to the LPA, however, whether and what enforcement action they take against reported breaches.

The government advises LPAs to "act proportionately" in responding to breaches.

Role of the Local Government Ombudsman

If constituents have concerns about the way in which an LPA took a planning decision or about a lack of enforcement action by an LPA, they can complain to the Local Government Ombudsman. A local authority's own complaints procedure must first have been exhausted for the Ombudsman to look at a case. The Ombudsman can only look at whether the LPA followed correct processes. They cannot overturn a planning decision. If they find fault with an LPA's procedures, the Ombudsman will issue recommendations to the LPA about how it can improve.

UK's Levelling-up and Regeneration Act 2023: Proposed Key Changes to the Planning System

We mentioned above that there has been a change in the law that is intended to free up the planning system in the UK. The planning system is a complex and evolving topic. The UK government, in the White Paper, Planning for the Future, proposed a new planning system that is easier for the public to access, transforms the way communities are shaped, and builds the homes this country needs. It is the view that the current planning system is complex and slows up development. The government's White Paper proposed the most radical reforms to the planning system in decades. This resulted in The Levelling-up and Regeneration Act 2023. The UK government states that the Act will "speed up the planning system, hold developers to account, cut bureaucracy, and encourage more councils to put in place plans to enable the building of new homes."

Many of the measures set out in the Act are not fully detailed (further regulations are required before they can take effect) and, while the changes are intended to simplify the planning regime, developers should closely follow the progress of implementing legislation over the coming months.

The Act largely provides a framework for a raft of future changes to the planning system. Many of these intended changes will first require the introduction of secondary legislation and new planning policy before they can take effect.

Commencement Notices for Planning Permissions

Before commencing development pursuant to planning permission, a developer will be required to submit a commencement notice to the local planning authority specifying the date on which the development is expected to begin. Failure to serve a notice will be a criminal offence liable on summary conviction to a fine of up to £1,000.

Developers will need to comply with this new requirement. The mandatory commencement notices will provide a formal record of when development commenced.

Changes to the Roles of the Development Plan and National Policy in Determining a Planning Application

Section 94 of the new Act introduces the concept of National Development Management Policies ("NDMP"), which will be national development and land use policies covering issues of general application across most areas (for example, heritage protection). These policies will be subject to consultation and are to be determined by the secretary of state.

Section 93 of the Act changes the roles of the local development plan and national planning policy in determining a planning application. If regard is to be had to the local development plan and any NDMP, the determination must be in accordance with the development plan and the NDMP, taken together, unless material considerations strongly indicate otherwise. However, if there is any conflict between a development plan and a NDMP, then the conflict must be resolved in favour of the NDMP. *The long-established statutory primacy of the development plan is therefore eroded.*

New Section 73B for "Permission Not Substantially Different for Existing Permission"

The Act inserts a new section 73B into the Town and Country Planning Act 1990 ("TCPA") for *"Applications for permission not substantially different from existing permission."* This is intended to help plug the gap between applying for wholly new planning permissions and the sometimes-necessary practice of using two applications, one for "non-material amendments" under section 96A of the TCPA 1990 and one for "minor material amendments" under section 73 of the TCPA 1990, in order to secure amendments to proposed development schemes.

The practice of submitting parallel applications arose following the *Finney* judgment, In the case of John Leslie Finney v Welsh Ministers & Carmarthenshire County Council, Energiekontor (Uk) Limited (otherwise known as "Finney") the Courts established that an application under s73 may not be used to obtain a permission that would require a variation to the terms of the "operative" part of the planning permission, that is, the description of the development for which the original permission was granted.

Section 73B will come with certain limitations. For example, it cannot be used in respect of a planning permission granted under section 73 or 73A, and it cannot be used to alter the time limits for beginning work or for submitting reserved matters applications.

10-Year Time Limit for All Enforcement Action in England

The Act amends section 171B of the TCPA 1990 to extend the enforcement time limits for a breach of planning control comprising building without planning permission and change of use to a single dwellinghouse from four to 10 years. The abolition of the four-year rule for these breaches of planning control applies to England only (the four-year rule still applies in Wales).

New Infrastructure Levy Set to Replace CIL

The Act introduces a new charge on development called the Infrastructure Levy ("IL").

All local planning authorities in England will be mandated to issue an IL charging schedule, rather than having discretion to do so as is currently the case with the Community Infrastructure Levy ("CIL"). The Infrastructure Levy would be based on the gross development value rather than the development's floorspace. The IL liability would be paid as and when the relevant development commences and in accordance with procedures to be set out in the IL regulations.

IL is intended to fund affordable housing as well as other local infrastructure and should reduce the circumstances in which a section 106 agreement is required. Section 106 agreements are legal agreements between a planning authority and a developer, or undertakings offered unilaterally by a developer, that ensure that certain extra works related to a development are undertaken.

IL is also intended to replace CIL in due course (save for Mayoral CIL in Greater London and CIL in Wales, which will remain).

Until further regulations are issued by the secretary of state, there is some uncertainty as to how IL will interact with the existing CIL regimes and section 106 obligations.

Further proposed developments in 2024

Before the election of the Labour Government in July 2024, the Housing Secretary, Michael Gove, had suggested further changes to the planning system in a bid to accelerate developments. One change was to extend so called 'permitted development rights'. Now, planning permission is required to convert office spaces larger than 15,00 square feet into homes. This cap was set to be scrapped. Also, it was proposed that there will be an acceleration of development on suitable Brownfield sites.

As we saw in the introduction, the Labour government is set to introduce changes to enable more rapid development of houses, and a reduction of the obstacles seen to prevent this.

Planning differences in Scotland Wales and Northern Ireland

Scotland:

Scotland has its own devolved planning system governed by the Scottish Parliament. Key features include:

- **National Planning Framework (NPF)**: Sets out Scotland's long-term spatial strategy, guiding development and land use.
- **Local Development Plans (LDPs)**: Prepared by local authorities, these plans outline policies for specific areas.
- **Development Management**: Local authorities handle planning applications and enforce regulations.
- **Community Engagement**: Scotland emphasizes community involvement in planning decisions.
- **Environmental Impact Assessments (EIAs)**: Required for certain developments.
- **Scottish Planning Policy (SPP)**: Provides national planning guidance.
- For further information on the Scottish Planning system go to: www.gov.scot/policies/planning-architecture.

Wales:

The **Welsh Government** oversees planning in Wales. Key aspects include:

- **Planning (Wales) Act 2015**: Introduced significant reforms, emphasizing sustainable development, community engagement, and well-being.
- **National Development Framework (NDF)**: Sets out Wales' spatial priorities.
- **Local Development Plans (LDPs)**: Prepared by local authorities, aligning with NDF goals.
- **Designated Landscapes**: Wales protects its natural and cultural heritage through designated landscapes.
- **Community Right to Build Orders**: Empower communities to shape local development.
- **Welsh National Marine Plan**: Guides marine development.

For further information on the Welsh Planning system go to: www.planningportal.co.uk/wales/planning/about-the-planning-system/local-plans

Northern Ireland:

Northern Ireland's planning system has recently undergone changes.

Key features include:

- **Local Councils**: Planning functions were transferred to local councils.
- **Strategic Planning Policy Statement (SPPS)**: Provides overarching guidance.
- **Local Development Plans (LDPs)**: Prepared by councils, focusing on local needs.
- **Development Management**: Councils handle planning applications.
- **Community Involvement**: Public participation is encouraged.
- **Environmental Impact Assessments (EIAs)**: Required for certain projects.

For further information on the Northern Ireland Planning System go to:

www.nidirect.gov.uk/services/planning-portal.

Common Themes:

The planning systems in the UK emphasize sustainable development, community engagement, and environmental considerations. National or Regional Planning Policy Frameworks provide long-term guidance

In summary, while each nation tailors its planning system to its unique context, they share a commitment to shaping their environments for the benefit of present and future generations.

In Part 2 overleaf, we will now look at the different planning use classes as they relate to different types of development.

****

Part 2

What are Planning Use Classes?

> As we saw in Part 1, Planning ensures that the right development happens in the right place at the right time, benefitting communities and the economy. It plays a critical role in identifying what development is needed and where, what areas need to be protected or enhanced and in assessing whether proposed development is suitable. In Part 2, we will look at the system of Planning Use Classes.

Planning Use Classes

The Town and Country Planning (Use Classes) Order 1987 (as amended) puts uses of land and buildings into various categories known as 'Use Classes'. It was amended following the 2015 Use Classes Amendment Order and further radical changes were introduced with effect from 1st September 2020.

The general rule is that planning permission is not required to move between uses within the same Use Class.

As the table overleaf shows, the 2020 overhaul of planning use classes made it possible, without planning permission being required, to switch from a shop to an office. However, for a school to change to day nursery planning permission is now required. Sui generis means of a kind on its own i.e. a property with sui generis use does not fall into any Use Class so planning permission is required to change the use.

The following list (overleaf) gives an indication of the types of use that may fall within each use class. You should note that this is a guide only and local planning authorities will determine, in the first instance, which use class a particular use falls into.

What are Planning Use Classes?

Category	Description
E	Shops, retail warehouses, hairdressers, undertakers, travel and ticket agencies, post offices (but not sorting offices), pet shops, sandwich bars, showrooms, domestic hire shops, dry cleaners, funeral directors and internet cafes.
E	Financial services such as banks and building societies, professional services (other than health and medical services) including estate and employment agencies and betting offices.
E	For the sale of food and drink for consumption on the premises - restaurants, snack bars and cafes.
Sui Generis	Public houses, wine bars or other drinking establishments (but not nightclubs).
Sui Generis	For the sale of hot food for consumption off the premises.
E	Offices (other than those that fall within A2), research and

	development of products and processes, light industry appropriate in a residential area.
B2	Use for industrial process other than one falling within class B1 (excluding incineration purposes, chemical treatment or landfill or hazardous waste).
B8	This class includes openair storage.
C2	Residential care homes, hospitals, nursing homes, boarding schools, residential colleges and training centres.
C2A	Use for the provision of secure residentialaccommodation, including use as a prison, young offenders institution, detention centre, secure training centre, custody centre, short-term holding centre, secure hospital, secure local authority accommodation or use as a military barracks.

C3	C3(C3 (a) covers use by a single person or a family (a couple whether married or not, a person related to one another with members of the family of one of the couple to be treated as members of the family of the other), an employer and certain domestic employees (such as an au pair, nanny, nurse, governess, servant, chauffeur, gardener, secretary and personal assistant), a carer and the person receiving the care and a foster parent and foster child.
	C3(b): up to six people living together as a single household and receiving care e.g. supported housing schemes such as those for people with learning disabilities or mental health problems.
	C3(c) allows for groups of people (up to six) living together as a single household. This allows for those groupings that do not fall within the C4 HMO definition, but which fell within the previous C3 use class, to be provided for i.e. a small religious

	community may fall into this section as could a homeowner who is living with a lodger.
C4	Small shared dwelling houses occupied by between three and six unrelated individuals, as their only or main residence, who share basic amenities such as a kitchen or bathroom.
E	Clinics, health centres, crèches, day nurseries and day centres.
F1	Schools, art galleries (other than for sale or hire), museums, libraries, public halls, places of worship and law court. Non-residential education and training centres.
Sui Generis	Cinemas, music and concert halls,

What are Planning Use Classes?

	bingo and dance halls (but not nightclubs)
E	Gymnasiums or areas for indoor sports and recreations (except for motor sports, or where firearms are used).
F2	Indoor or outdoor swimming pools and skating rinks. Outdoor sports and recreation not involving motorised vehicles or firearms.
F2	Hall or meeting place for the principal use of the local community.
Sui Generis	Certain uses do not fall within any use class and are considered 'sui generis'. Such uses include: theatres, houses in multiple occupation, hostels providing no significant element of care, scrap yards. Petrol filling stations and shops selling and/or displaying motor vehicles. Retail warehouse clubs, nightclubs, launderettes, taxi businesses amusement centres and casinos.

Before you negotiate a lease or buy a property for your business, check whether you need to obtain planning permission for your intended use, and, if so, your chances of getting it.

Permitted development - change from commercial to residential

Since 2013 premises in office use (previously classified as B1(a)) can change to C3 residential use, subject to Prior Approval covering flooding, highways and transport issues and contamination. The property must have been either in use as an office before 30th May 2013 or if vacant at that date have been last used as an office. Some local authorities have imposed restrictions known as Article 4 Declarations removing such rights. There are also permitted development rights in relation to converting industrial and retail property to residential, subject to Prior Approval.

Certificate of Lawful Use

If a property can be demonstrated to have been in residential use for a minimum period of four years it may be possible to obtain a Certificate of Lawful use which will confirm the property effectively has planning permission for that use. For commercial properties, the period is ten years.

What are Planning Use Classes?

Proposed changes to planning use for intended Airbnb use

Airbnb owners may soon need planning consent. The then Housing Secretary Michael Gove (until July 2024) had announced proposals to require planning permission for short-term lets such as Airbnb, to prevent a "hollowing out" of communities. The new law would require people letting out properties as a short-term holiday home in England to seek permission from the local authority under a new "use" category. The rules would not apply to people renting out their main home for 90 days or fewer in a year. A mandatory register would be set up providing English councils with information on lets in their area. Mr. Gove, the then Secretary of State for Levelling Up, Housing and Communities, said: "We know short-term let's can be helpful for the tourist economy, but we are now giving councils the tools to bring them under control so that local people can rent those homes as well. "These changes strike a balance between giving local people access to more affordable housing, while ensuring the visitor economy continues to flourish."

In Part 3 overleaf, we will look at the processes involved in making a planning application.

****

Part 3

Obtaining Planning Permission

> *In Part 1, we discussed the planning system generally within the context of planning laws and we also discussed permitted developments. In Part 2, we discussed the practice of Planning use Classes.*
>
> *Although the planning systems are similar in each country in the UK, nevertheless there are differences in emphasis and procedure.*
>
> *For more information about the planning system in Wales, Scotland and Northern Ireland you should visit:*
> - *www.gov.wales/planning-permission*
> - *www.mygov.scot/planning-permission (Scotland)*
> - *www.nidirect.gov.uk/information-and-services/repairs-planning-and-building-regulations/planning-system (Northern Ireland)*

Planning permission generally

The construction of new buildings and extensive changes to existing buildings will usually require consent from the local planning authority in the form of planning permission. In a nutshell, the planning system is intended to control inappropriate development. For details of your local authority, you should go to www.planningportal.co.uk. where you can begin the process of obtaining planning permission.

Adding outbuildings or building extensions requires planning permission depending on the size of the project and the level of Permitted Development rights afforded to or still remaining on a property. See Part 6 for more on permitted development rights and specific projects.

Briefly, the policy of Permitted Development was introduced at the very beginning of the planning system – in the Town and Planning Act 1948, on 1st July 1948 – and allows for minor improvements, such as converting a loft or modest extensions to your home, to be undertaken without clogging up the planning system. Scotland, Wales and Northern Ireland each benefit from their own version of these rules. You should visit the websites outlined above.

The level of work that can be carried out under Permitted Development depends on a variety of factors including location (Areas of Natural Beauty and Conservation Areas have different rules), and the extent of work already carried out on a property.

The most important point when it comes to obtaining planning permission, whether outline or full, is that you will need, in most cases, to use an architect. Only very skilled and knowledgeable people can manage without one.

Architects will let you know what they would charge for taking on the project and steer you through the design process, along with making the planning application. They will also deal with building control issues. In addition, if necessary, they can arrange for a topographical survey and also deal with the local utilities, such as water authorities who need to provide clearance before you can build.

There are many issues when seeking to obtain planning permission to construct or alter a property. The most important ones will be advised by the architects, such as access, light, building control issues and so on.

The process of applying for planning permission
Types of planning application

There are 2 main types of planning application – applications for full planning permission and applications for outline planning permission. Applications can also be made for:
- approval of reserved matters;

- discharge of conditions;
- amending proposals that have planning permission;
- amending planning obligations;
- lawful development certificates;
- prior approval for some permitted development rights;
- non-planning consents (such as advertisement consent, consent required under a Tree Preservation Order and hazardous substances consent).

Non-planning consents

Non-planning consents are those consents that may have to be obtained alongside or after, and separate from, planning permission in order to complete and operate a development lawfully.

Application for full planning permission

An application for full planning permission results in a decision on the detailed proposals of how a site can be developed. If planning permission is granted, and subject to compliance with any planning conditions that are imposed, no further engagement with the local planning authority is required to proceed with the development granted permission, although other consents may be required.

Outline planning application

An application for outline planning permission allows for a decision on the general principles of how a site can be developed. Outline planning permission is granted subject to conditions requiring the subsequent approval of one or more reserved matters.

What are reserved matters?

Reserved matters are those aspects of a proposed development which an applicant can choose not to submit details of with an outline planning application, (i.e. they can be 'reserved' for later determination).

These are defined in article 2 of the Town and Country Planning (Development Management Procedure) (England) Order 2015 as:

- 'Access' – the accessibility to and within the site, for vehicles, cycles and pedestrians in terms of the positioning and treatment of access and circulation routes and how these fit into the surrounding access network.
- 'Appearance' – the aspects of a building or place within the development which determine the visual impression the building or place makes, including the external built form of the development, its architecture, materials, decoration, lighting, colour and texture.

- 'Landscaping' – the treatment of land (other than buildings) for the purpose of enhancing or protecting the amenities of the site and the area in which it is situated and includes: (a) screening by fences, walls or other means; (b) the planting of trees, hedges, shrubs or grass; (c) the formation of banks, terraces or other earthworks; (d) the laying out or provision of gardens, courts, squares, water features, sculpture or public art; and (e) the provision of other amenity features;
- 'Layout' – the way in which buildings, routes and open spaces within the development are provided, situated and orientated in relation to each other and to buildings and spaces outside the development.
- 'Scale' – the height, width and length of each building proposed within the development in relation to its surroundings.

Under section 92 of the Town and Country Planning Act 1990, applications for approval of reserved matters must be made within a specified time-limit, normally 3 years from the date outline planning permission was granted.

Applications for approval under outline permission may be made either for all reserved matters at once, or individually. Even after details relating to a particular reserved matter have been approved, one or more fresh applications can be made for approval of alternative details in relation to the same reserved matter. Once the time-limit for applications for approval of reserved matters has expired, however, no applications for such an approval may be submitted.

Which authority should deal with a planning application
Most planning applications are submitted to the relevant local planning authority.

In 2-tier council areas the relevant local planning authority will be the district council, except for applications involving minerals and waste development which are made to the county council.
In certain limited cases, it is possible to make an application direct to the Planning Inspectorate.

Land in more than one local planning authority area
Where a site which is the subject of a planning application straddles one or more local planning authority boundaries, the applicant must submit identical applications to each local planning authority.

Development to be undertaken by a local authority

The procedures dealing with development proposed by local authorities are contained in the Town and Country Planning General Regulations 1992 (as amended). The principle underlying these Regulations is that local authorities must make planning applications in the same way as any other person and must follow the same procedures as would apply to applications by others.

Local authorities may grant themselves planning permission for their own development on land in which they have an interest or for development by an authority jointly with another person.

The proposals must be publicised in the same way as any similar application from any other applicant and they cannot be decided by a committee or officer responsible for the management of any land or buildings to which the application relates.

Local authority development proposals, like those of other persons applying for planning permission, must be determined in accordance with the development plan unless material considerations indicate otherwise. Planning permission which any local authority grants to itself runs with the land.

Development to be undertaken by the Crown

The Crown must make applications for planning permission, listed building consent and hazardous substances consent in the same way as applications made by any other party. The exception is an application for urgent Crown development made under section 293A of the Town and Country Planning Act 1990.

What kinds of application are made directly to the Planning Inspectorate?

- Applications for development consent for Nationally Significant Infrastructure.
- Applications for urgent Crown development.
- Applications for major development under section 62A of the 1990 Act where the local planning authority has been designated by the Secretary of State and the applicant has chosen to submit an application to the Planning Inspectorate.

The Department for Business, Energy & Industrial Strategy (BEIS) administers the provisions of the Electricity Act 1989 for developers seeking consents from the Secretary of State for the construction of overhead lines. This applies to overhead lines with a nominal voltage of less than 132 kilovolts and lines with a nominal voltage of 132 kilovolts or greater that are under 2 kilometres in length.

Validation requirements

Requirements to make a valid application for planning permission

The submission of a valid application for planning permission requires:

(a) a completed application form
(b) compliance with national information requirements
(c) the correct application fee
(d) provision of local information requirements

Where can the standard application form be found?

Applicants are encouraged to apply electronically through the local planning authority's website. The standard application form can be viewed for information at Planning application and fire statement forms: templates. Alternatively, an application can be completed on a paper version of the form provided by the local planning authority. Most applications can be made using the standard application form. The standard application form cannot currently be used for applications for mining operations or the use of land for mineral-working deposits, although there is a separate paper form for onshore oil and gas development. Applications made under the Planning (Hazardous Substances) Act 1990 for hazardous substance consent are also not covered by the Standard Application Form. Such applications must be made on a form provided by the local planning authority.

Making a planning application on paper

Applicants are encouraged to apply electronically. However, online submission of supporting information may not always be possible. In these circumstances, information can be submitted to the local planning authority in hard copy, or electronically (e.g. on a CD or USB storage device).

For electronic applications, a typed signature of the applicant or agent's name is acceptable.

Copies of the application form

Applications submitted electronically do not need to be accompanied by any further copies either of the application or accompanying information.

Applicants who apply on a paper copy of the standard application form must provide the original plus 3 copies of the form (a total of 4 copies), unless the local planning authority indicates that a smaller number is required.

Local planning authorities may request additional copies above the statutory requirement, but failure to provide these additional copies would not be a basis for refusing to validate the application.

A local planning authority cannot refuse to validate an application if an applicant who has made an application electronically does not provide paper copies. Similarly, a local planning authority cannot refuse to validate an application if an applicant does not provide an electronic copy of the application.

The Community Infrastructure Levy

The Community Infrastructure Levy means that authorities charging the levy require additional information to determine whether a charge is due and to determine the amount. Applicants are required to answer additional questions to enable authorities to calculate levy liability.

National information requirements
- An application for planning permission must be accompanied by:
- Plans and drawings.
- Ownership Certificate and Agricultural Land Declaration.

- Design and Access Statement (for some planning applications).
- Fire Statement (for some planning applications made on or after 1 August 2021)
- In addition, there are specific requirements in relation to:
- Outline planning applications.
- Applications that are subject to Environmental Impact Assessment.

Plans and drawings

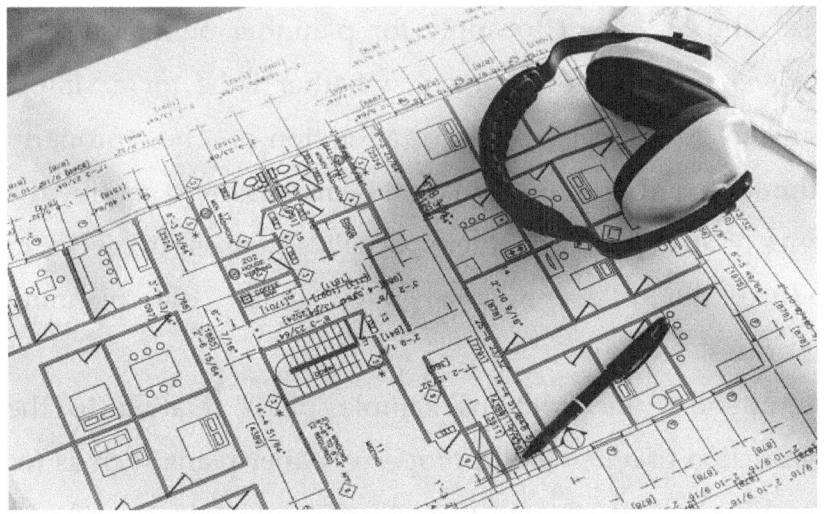

As a minimum, applicants will need to submit a 'location plan' that shows the application site in relation to the surrounding area. Additional plans and drawings will in most cases be necessary to describe the proposed development, as required by the legislation (see article 7(1)(c)(ii) of the Town and Country Planning (Development Management Procedure (England) (Order) 2015. These may be requested by the local planning authority through their local list of information requirements, where it is reasonable to do so.

Any plans or drawings must be drawn to an identified scale, and in the case of plans, must show the direction of north. Although not a requirement of legislation, the inclusion of a linear scale bar is also useful, particularly in the case of electronic submissions.

At this point, as we have stated, it is worth reminding those who are about to apply for planning permission, for whatever type of development, whether it be for a simple extension or the construction or alteration of a new property or thinking of doing so, that it will be necessary to employ the service of an architect or other specialists such as surveyors, to produce the plans necessary to satisfy the planning authorities.

Appendix one contains sample plans relating to the construction of a new build property. Other plans such as for extending a property will need to be drafted in accordance with planning authority requirement.

See overleaf for an example of a simple home extension plan.

PROPOSED SIDE ELEVATION

PROPOSED REAR ELEVATION

PROPOSED FRONT ELEVATION

PROPOSED SIDE ELEVATION

What information should be included on a location plan?

A location plan should be based on an up-to-date map. The scale should typically be 1:1250 or 1:2500, but wherever possible the plan should be scaled to fit onto A4 or A3 size paper. A location plan should identify sufficient roads and/or buildings on land adjoining the application site to ensure that the exact location of the application site is clear.

The application site should be edged clearly with a red line on the location plan. It should include all land necessary to carry out the proposed development (e.g. land required for access to the site from a public highway, visibility splays, landscaping, car parking and open areas around buildings). A blue line should be drawn around any other land owned by the applicant, close to or adjoining the application site.

Ownership Certificate and Agricultural Land Declaration

A certificate which applicants must complete provides certain details about the ownership of the application site and confirms that an appropriate notice has been served on any other owners (and agricultural tenants). The forms of notice are in Schedule 2 to the Town and Country Planning (Development Management Procedure) (England) (Order) 2015.

An application is not valid, and therefore cannot be determined by the local planning authority, unless the relevant certificate has been completed. It is an offence to complete a false or misleading certificate, either knowingly or recklessly, with a maximum fine of up to £5,000.

Four categories of ownership certificate

- **Certificate A – Sole Ownership and no agricultural tenants** This should only be completed if the applicant is the sole owner of the land to which the application relates and there are no agricultural tenants.
- **Certificate B – Shared Ownership (All other owners/agricultural tenants known)** This should be completed if the applicant is not the sole owner, or if there are agricultural tenants, and the applicant knows the names and addresses of all the other owners and/or agricultural tenants.
- **Certificate C – Shared Ownership (Some other owners/agricultural tenants known)** This should be completed if the applicant does not own all of the land to which the application relates and does not know the name and address of all of the owners and/or agricultural tenants.

- **Certificate D – Shared Ownership (None of the other owners/agricultural tenants known)** This should be completed if the applicant does not own all of the land to which the application relates and does not know the names and addresses of any of the owners and/or agricultural tenants.

An 'owner' is anyone with a freehold interest, or leasehold interest the unexpired term of which is not less than 7 years. In the case of development consisting of the winning or working of minerals, a person entitled to an interest in a mineral in the land is also an owner. An 'agricultural tenant' is a tenant of an agricultural holding, any part of which is comprised in the land to which the application relates.

Any hard copy certificate submitted with the standard application form must be signed by hand. For any electronically submitted certificate, a typed signature of the applicant's name is acceptable. Ownership certificates must also be completed for applications for listed building consent, although no agricultural declaration is required.

Making a planning application for someone else's land

The planning system entitles anyone to apply for permission to develop any plot of land, irrespective of ownership.

However, an applicant is required to notify owners of the land or buildings to which the application relates, as well as any agricultural tenants, in accordance with article 13 of the Town and Country Planning (Development Management Procedure) (England) Order 2015. When making an application, an applicant is required to sign a certificate confirming the ownership of the land to which the application relates and that the relevant notices have been served.

What is an agricultural land declaration?

All agricultural tenants on a site must be notified prior to the submission of an application for planning permission. Applicants must certify that they have notified any agricultural tenants about their application, or that there are no agricultural tenants on the site. This declaration is required whether or not the site includes an agricultural holding. It is incorporated into the ownership certificates on the standard application form.

Design and Access Statement

A Design and Access Statement is a concise report accompanying certain applications for planning permission and applications for listed building consent. They provide a framework for applicants to explain how the proposed development is a suitable response to the site and its setting and demonstrate that it can be adequately accessed by prospective users. Design and Access Statements can aid decision-making by enabling local planning authorities and third parties to better understand the analysis that has underpinned the design of a development proposal.

The level of detail in a Design and Access Statement should be proportionate to the complexity of the application but should not be overly long.

Applications to accompany a Design and Access Statement
- Applications for major development, as defined in article 2 of the Town and Country Planning (Development Management Procedure (England) Order 2015;
- Applications for development in a designated area, where the proposed development consists of:
    - one or more dwellings; or
    - a building or buildings with a floor space of 100 square metres or more.
- Applications for listed building consent.
- For the purposes of Design and Access Statements, a designated area means a World Heritage Site or a conservation area.

Applications for waste development, a material change of use, engineering or mining operations do not need to be accompanied by a Design and Access Statement.

Applications to amend the conditions attached to a planning permission do not need to be accompanied by a Design and Access Statement.

There are some differences between the requirements for applications for planning permission and applications for listed building consent.

What should be included in a Design and Access Statement?

A Design and Access Statement must:

(a) explain the design principles and concepts that have been applied to the proposed development; and

(b) demonstrate the steps taken to appraise the context of the proposed development, and how the design of the development takes that context into account.

A development's context refers to the particular characteristics of the application site and its wider setting. These will be specific to the circumstances of an individual application and a Design and Access Statement should be tailored accordingly.

Design and Access Statements must also explain the applicant's approach to access and how relevant Local Plan policies have been taken into account. They must detail any consultation undertaken in relation to access issues, and how the outcome of this consultation has informed the proposed development. Applicants must also explain how any specific issues which might affect access to the proposed development have been addressed.

Application for listed building consent
Design and Access Statements accompanying applications for listed building consent must include an explanation of the design principles and concepts that have been applied to the proposed works, and how they have taken account of:

- the special architectural or historic importance of the building;
- the particular physical features of the building that justify its designation as a listed building; and
- the building's setting.

Unless the proposed works only affect the interior of the building, Design and Access Statements accompanying applications for listed building consent must also explain how issues relating to access to the building have been dealt with. They must explain the applicant's approach to access, including what alternative means of access have been considered, and how relevant Local Plan policies have been taken into account. Statements must also explain how the applicant's approach to access takes account of matters (a)-(c) above.

Design and Access Statements accompanying applications for listed building consent must provide information on any consultation undertaken, and how the outcome of this consultation has informed the proposed works. Statements must also explain how any specific issues which might affect access to the building have been addressed.

Where a planning application is submitted in parallel with an application for listed building consent, a single, combined Design and Access Statement should address the requirements of both. The combined Statement should address the elements required in relation to a planning application and the additional requirements in relation to listed building consent.

Outline planning applications details

Information about the proposed use or uses, and the amount of development proposed for each use, is necessary to allow consideration of an application for outline planning permission. Under article 5(3) of the Development

Management Procedure Order 2015, an application for outline planning permission must also indicate the area or areas where access points to the development will be situated, even if access has been reserved.

Reserved matters with an outline application

An applicant can choose to submit details of any of the reserved matters as part of an outline application. Unless the applicant has indicated that those details are submitted "for illustrative purposes only" (or has otherwise indicated that they are not formally part of the application), the local planning authority must treat them as part of the development in respect of which the application is being made; the local planning authority cannot reserve that matter by condition for subsequent approval.

A local planning authority can request further details in relation to reserved matters under article 5(2) of the Town and Country Planning (Development Management Procedure) (England) Order 2015. If a local planning authority considers that an outline application ought to include details of the reserved matters it must notify the applicant no more than one month after the application is received, specifying which further details are required.

Environmental Impact Assessment

For projects requiring an Environmental Impact Assessment, an Environmental Statement (and non-technical summary) must be provided.

Local information requirements

Government policy on local information requirements

The government's policy on local information requirements can be found in the National Planning Policy Framework. Local planning authorities should take a proportionate approach to the information requested in support of planning applications.

A local planning authority may request supporting information with a planning application. Its requirements should be specified on a formally adopted 'local list' which has been published on its website less than 2 years before an application is submitted. Local information requirements have no bearing on whether a planning application is valid unless they are set out on such a list.

Receipt of an application

Once it has received an application, the local planning authority will register the application and send the applicant an acknowledgement that confirms the application has been

received and sets out the next steps. Issues that may arise when an application is first submitted:
- Changes to the description of the development
- Delay in validation of an application
- Dealing with 'repeat applications' for development that has already been refused

Changes to the description of development

Before publicising and consulting on an application, the local planning authority should be satisfied that the description of development provided by the applicant is accurate. The local planning authority should not amend the description of development without first discussing any revised wording with the applicant or their agent. Checking the accuracy of the description of development should not delay validation of an application.

Delay in the validation of an application

Applications should be validated as soon as practicable to allow the formal process of publicising and consulting on the application to begin. Sometimes delays can occur if there are concerns about the validity of an application.

In such circumstances, it is advisable for local planning authorities to:

- discuss their concerns with the applicant at the earliest opportunity; and
- give clear advice about what steps need to be taken to address their concerns.

The local planning authority will inform the applicant as soon as possible that this is the case, setting out what additional information it thinks needs to be provided. Any additional information must form part of the local list, and meet the statutory tests.

It is expected that both the applicant and local planning authority should make every effort to resolve disagreements about the information needed to support a planning application. Informal negotiation is clearly in the interests of both parties. The local planning authority should involve qualified planning officers in such discussions to judge what information is necessary.

Pre-application discussions can be a useful way for an applicant and local planning authority to agree what information is required before an application is submitted. This can help avoid disputes over the information necessary to validate an application and reduce associated delays.

There is a procedure in the Development Management Procedure Order to resolve such disputes. An applicant must first send the local planning authority a notice under article 12 of the Town and Country Planning (Development Management Procedure) (England) Order 2015 (an 'article 12 notice'). This must set out the reasons why the applicant considers that the information requested by the local planning authority, in refusing to validate the planning application, does not meet the statutory tests.

When a local planning authority receives an article 12 notice, it will consider the merits of the applicant's case as to why the information requested does not meet the statutory tests. The local planning authority must then either issue a 'validation notice', stating that it no longer requires the information specified in the article 12 notice, or a 'non-validation notice' stating that it still requires the applicant to provide the information requested.

A local planning authority must respond to an article 12 notice within the statutory time period for determining the application in question. Depending on the type of application, this would be 8, 13 or 16 weeks after the day the application is received, or an extended period agreed in writing between the applicant and local planning authority. Where possible, local planning authorities are encouraged to respond to such notices as soon as possible to facilitate further negotiations between the parties. If the statutory time period has already passed or will pass in 7 working days or less, the local planning authority must respond to the article 12 notice within 7 working days.

The article 12 procedure can apply to applications which are subject to Environmental Impact Assessment. However, they cannot be used to resolve disputes over information that is necessary to meet requirements under the Town and Country Planning (Environmental Impact Assessment) Regulations 2011.

Local planning authority has served a non-validation notice

After receiving a non-validation notice and after the relevant period has passed without the local planning authority granting or refusing to grant planning permission, an applicant may appeal to the Planning Inspectorate against non-determination of the application.

In such cases, the statutory time period will be considered to have begun at the point where the local planning authority has received the fee, documents and other information necessary to validate the application, but excluding the disputed information specified in the article 12 notice. The Planning Inspectorate will consider the merits of the validation dispute and the appeal itself.

If the local planning authority fails to respond to an article 12 notice or determine the application within the relevant time periods, the applicant has a right of appeal to the Planning Inspectorate against non-determination.

Application for a development already refused

An application can be made for a development that has already been refused. However local planning authorities have the power to decline an application for planning permission which is similar to an application that, within the last 2 years, has been dismissed by the Secretary of State on appeal or refused following call-in.

A local planning authority may also decline to determine an application for planning permission if it has refused more than one similar application within the last 2 years and there has been no appeal to the Secretary of State. In declining to determine an application, a local planning authority must be of the view that there has been no significant change in the development plan (so far as relevant to the application) and any other material considerations since the similar application was refused or dismissed on appeal. This power includes the ability to decline to determine applications for listed building consent and applications for the prior approval of a local planning authority for development which is permitted under the Town and Country Planning (General Permitted Development) Order 2015. Where a local planning authority declines to determine an application, it should notify the applicant that it has exercised its power under section 70A of the Town and Country Planning Act 1990, or section 81A of the Planning (Listed Buildings and Conservation Areas) Act 1990, to decline to determine the application and should return the application to the applicant.

Where an authority considers that an application is similar, it is not automatically obliged to decline to determine the application. The purpose of these powers is to inhibit the use of 'repeat' applications that the local planning authority believes are submitted with the intention of, over time, wearing down opposition to proposed developments. They are, however, designed to be flexible and to give local planning authorities the discretion to entertain 'repeat' planning applications where they are satisfied that a genuine attempt has been made to overcome the planning objections which led to rejection of the previous proposal or there has been a material change in circumstances.

Changes after validation of an application

It is possible for an applicant to suggest changes to an application before the local planning authority has determined the proposal. It is equally possible after the consultation period for the local planning authority to ask the applicant if it would be possible to revise the application to overcome a possible objection. It is at the discretion of the local planning authority whether to accept such changes, to determine if the changes need to be reconsulted upon, or if the proposed changes are so significant as to materially alter the proposal such that a new application should be submitted.

Appealing against a planning decision

You can appeal a planning decision if any of the following apply:

- you were refused planning permission for reasons that you think go against the LPA's development plan or planning policy (you can usually find these on their website)
- you were granted planning permission with conditions you object to - you'll need to explain why you think they're unnecessary, unenforceable, vague, unreasonable or irrelevant
- the LPA has not given you a decision on your application and 8 weeks have passed since the date they told you they'd received it (or a different deadline you agreed with them has passed)

For major projects, you can only appeal if 13 weeks have passed. Examples of a major project include a development with 10 or more dwellings, or a building with floor space of more than 1,000 square metres.

Use the appeal a householder planning decision service:

www.gov.uk/appeal-householder-planning-decision.

If you want to appeal a refused application for a smaller project, like an extension, conservatory or loft conversion.

You can also appeal a listed building consent decision.

Who can appeal

You can appeal a decision for an application you made yourself, or appeal on behalf of someone else. You'll be asked to provide the planning application number and decision date. You can also comment on an appeal.

Applying for costs

You can apply for an 'award of costs' if you believe the LPA has cost you money by behaving unreasonably. For example, if you think their behaviour has caused you to miss a deadline. The LPA can also apply to get costs from you.

How long you have to appeal

If your application was refused, or granted with conditions, you can appeal for up to 6 months from the date on your local planning authority's (LPA) decision letter.

If you have not received a decision, you can appeal for up to 6 months from the date your decision was due to arrive.

Enforcement notices

You'll have less time to appeal if you received an enforcement notice in the last 2 years. If you received the enforcement notice before your application was refused, you have 28 days from the date on your decision letter to appeal. If the enforcement notice came after your application was refused, you need to appeal by whichever of these dates is sooner:

- 28 days from the date you received the enforcement notice
- 6 months from the date on your application decision letter

Fees

There's no fee for appealing.

Documents you need-Your appeal statement

You'll need to create an appeal statement. This is a document that explains why you're appealing. It's sometimes called a statement of case. For a full example of the appeal process plus sample forms go to:

www.gov.uk/government/publications/planning-appeals-how-to-complete-your-appeal-form/making-your-appeal-how-to-complete-your-planning-appeal-form

Copies

You'll need to submit copies of:
- your planning application form
- the decision letter from the local planning authority (LPA), if you have one
- all plans, drawings and documents you sent to the LPA in your application
- the site plan for your appeal site
- the ownership certificate document, if you submitted one separately as part of your application

If you're requesting a hearing or public inquiry

You also need to create a draft statement of common ground. This is a document explaining the parts of your planning application that you believe the local planning department will not disagree with.

Preparing your documents

You can submit the documents as any of these file types, as long as they're smaller than 15MB:

- DOC or DOCX
- JPG or JPEG
- PDF
- PNG
- TIF or TIFF

Make sure all documents are fully readable without any redacted text.

The planning register

Article 40 of the Town and Country Planning (Development Management Procedure) (England) Order 2015 requires each local planning authority to maintain a register of planning applications in relation to their area.

The planning register is held at the local planning authority's offices. Article 40(14) of the Town and Country Planning (Development Management Procedure) (England) Order 2015 makes provision for the register to be made available online.

Subject to meeting the requirements of article 40 of the Town and Country Planning (Development Management

Procedure) (England) Order 2015 and the Town and Country Planning (Environmental Impact Assessment) Regulations 2017 it is for local planning authorities to decide what information they include on the planning register.

In 2-tier areas it is only the district which must keep the planning register; the county is under no duty to keep a planning register. Under article 11(4) of the Town and Country Planning Development Management Procedure (England) Order 2015, a copy of any application made to the county, as well as accompanying plans, drawings and information, must be sent to the district by the county. Hard copies or electronic copies are acceptable. Copies sent electronically must meet the requirements of article 2(3) of the Town and Country Planning (Development Management Procedure) (England) Order 2015.

Costs of applying for planning permission

The fee for submitting a planning application varies depending on the nature of the development. The cost is currently £624 (2024) for a full application for a new single dwelling in England, but this fee is different in Scotland, Wales and Northern Ireland. For home improvers, an application in England for an extension currently costs £258, whereas in Wales the cost of a typical householder application is currently £198.

For a full breakdown of fees go to: www.planningportal.co.uk.

As well as fees for pre-application advice, further small sums are payable for the discharge of 'planning conditions' which must be met before development begins.

See overleaf for a simple summary of the planning process.

A Brief **Summary of the planning process**

```
┌─────────────────────────────────────────────────────────────────┐
│              PLANNING APPLICATION SUBMITTED                      │
└─────────────────────────────────────────────────────────────────┘
                              │
┌─────────────────────────────────────────────────────────────────┐
│    COUNCIL CHECKS WHETHER THE APPLICATION IS VALID AND           │
│           REQUESTS ANY MISSING PAPERWORK                         │
└─────────────────────────────────────────────────────────────────┘
                              │
┌─────────────────────────────────────────────────────────────────┐
│       COUNCIL ACKNOWLEDGES THE APPLICATION IS VALID              │
└─────────────────────────────────────────────────────────────────┘
                              │
┌─────────────────────────────────────────────────────────────────┐
│   COUNCIL PUBLICISES APPLICATION IN ACCORDANCE WITH ITS          │
│   POLICY AND WRITES TO ANY STATUTORY CONSULTEES (E.G.            │
│                   ENVIRONMENT AGENCY)                            │
└─────────────────────────────────────────────────────────────────┘
                              │
┌─────────────────────────────────────────────────────────────────┐
│       COUNCIL PLANNING OFFICERS WRITE A REPORT WITH              │
│                    RECOMMENDATIONS                               │
└─────────────────────────────────────────────────────────────────┘
                              │
┌─────────────────────────────────────────────────────────────────┐
│  COUNCIL'S DELEGATION SCHEME SETS OUT WHO SHOULD MAKE THE        │
│                         DECISION                                 │
└─────────────────────────────────────────────────────────────────┘
                              │
                    PLANNING COMMITTEE
                       ┌──────────┐
                       │ DECISION │
                       └──────────┘

REFUSE_____
GRANT WITH
CONDITIONS
```

Part 4

Building Regulations and the Role of Building Inspectors

> *It can be seen, in chapter 3, that the planning process is indeed long and convoluted. The fact that an architect or other specialist needs to be involved also makes it quite costly. However, that isn't the end of bureaucracy! Following granting of planning permission, there is now the issue of dealing with building regulations and building inspectors.*
>
> *See below for a full outline of building regulations and what this entails.*

Building regulations as at 2024

Building regulations in the United Kingdom are statutory regulations that seek to ensure that the policies set out in the relevant legislation are carried out. It is important to note that Building regulations approval is required for most building work in the UK. Obtaining planning permission is only the beginning.

Building regulations that apply across England and Wales are set out in the Building Act 1984, as amended, while those that apply across Scotland are set out in the Building (Scotland) Act 2003.

The regulations made under the Act have been periodically updated, rewritten or consolidated, with the current version being the Building Regulations 2010. The Building Regulations 2010 have recently been updated by the Building Safety Act 2022 (c. 30). In addition, there have been changes to building regulations in 2024, some of which have been in response to the Grenfell fire.

They are as follows:

Building Control Process for Higher-Risk Buildings:
- The **Building (Higher-Risk Buildings Procedures) (England) Regulations 2023** introduce a new building control process for higher-risk buildings. This process applies to multi-occupied residential buildings, hospitals, and care homes that are at least 18 meters in height or have at least 7 storeys. The process is overseen by the Building Safety Regulator.
- These regulations align with the recommendations from Dame Judith Hackitt's *Building a Safer Future* report and aim to enhance safety standards in the design and construction of higher-risk buildings.

Wider Changes to Procedural Building Regulations:
- The **Building Regulations etc. (Amendment) (England) Regulations 2023** introduce changes that apply to all building work. These changes raise standards across the built environment.
- New homes are now required to produce around 30% less CO_2 than current standards, contributing to net-zero goals. Additionally, there's a 27% reduction in emissions from other new buildings.

Permitted Development Rights:
- Proposed amendments to certain rights allow for the upward extension of existing buildings and the demolition of certain buildings to rebuild as homes. These changes expand the scope of buildings that can benefit from these rights.

The UK Government is responsible for the relevant legislation and administration in England, the Welsh Government (at Cardiff) is the responsible body in Wales, the Scottish Government (at Edinburgh) is responsible for the issue in Scotland, and the Northern Ireland Executive (at Belfast) has responsibility within its jurisdiction. There are very similar (and technically very comparable) Building Regulations in the Republic of Ireland.

The detailed requirements of the Building Regulations in England and Wales are scheduled within 18 separate headings, each designated by a letter (Part A to Part R), and covering aspects such as workmanship, adequate materials, structure, waterproofing and weatherization, fire safety and means of escape, sound isolation, ventilation, safe (potable) water, protection from falling, drainage, sanitary facilities, accessibility and facilities for the disabled, electrical safety, security of a building, and high-speed broadband infrastructure.

For each Part, detailed specifications are available free online (in the English and Welsh governments' "approved documents") describing the matters to be taken into account. The approved documents are not literally legally binding in how the requirements must be met; rather, they present the expectation concerning minimum appropriate standards required for compliance with the Building Regulations, and the common methods and materials used to achieve these. The use of appropriate British Standards and/or European Standards is also accepted as one way of complying with the Building Regulations requirements.

However, the supply of gas (natural and/or LPG) is not controlled by the Building Regulations, as there are separate Gas Safety Regulations enforced by the Health and Safety Executive (HSE).

Newer versions of Building Regulations are generally not retrospective: they are applied to each new change or modification to a building (or new part of a building) but do not require renovation of existing elements.

There are general requirements for any change or improvement, that the building must not be left any less satisfactory in compliance than before the works, and areas worked on must not be left in unsafe conditions by reference to current standards. The Regulations may also specify in some cases, that when enough work is done in an area (such as partial new insulation) the remainder of that area must be brought to an appropriate standard; however, the standard required for an existing building may be less stringent than that required for a completely new building.

The Regulations also specify that some types of work must be undertaken by an appropriately qualified professional (such as works on gas or certain electrical matters), or must be notified to the relevant local authority's Building regulations approval for certification or approval.

The application of Building Regulations is separate and distinct from 'Town Planning' and 'planning permission'; the Building Regulations control how buildings are to be designed or modified on the public grounds of safety and sustainability while 'planning permission' is concerned with appropriate development, the nature of land usage, and the appearance of neighborhoods. Therefore, both must be considered when building works are to be undertaken.

Building regulations apply to the majority of construction works – even fairly minor alterations. Building regs are a set of standards designed to ensure a property is safe and comfortable to live in, and, increasingly, energy efficient and mitigating its contribution to carbon emissions.

Do I need building regulations approval?

if you intend to carry out any new structural work or alterations to your home, you will require building regulations approval, although in some of these cases, competent persons can self-certify their works for compliance:

- Drainage
- Heat-producing appliances
- Cavity wall insulation
- New electrics

All new homes need to adhere to building regulations too, and for this reason a building control inspector will visit at key stages of the build to inspect the work and ensure it complies. These stages include:
- Excavation for the building foundations
- Pouring concrete for the foundations
- Building the oversite
- Building the damp proof-course
- Drainage
- A visit prior to completion

A completion certificate will then be issued following the final inspection.

Which building regulations do I need to comply with?

Once you've secured your planning approval, the focus needs to shift to showing that your design ticks all the right technical boxes.

The main exemptions for building regulations are peripheral things such as small porches, conservatories or detached garages (up to 30m2 floor area).

The Approved Documents of the Building Regulations comprise of a series of detailed guidance manuals (ranging from A to S) covering everything from structure and fire safety through to security and electronic communications. The Regulations are very detailed, and can be read in full on the Communities and Local Government website:

www.gov.uk/government/organisations/ministry-of-housing-communities-local-government

In brief, your project will have to comply with these areas:
- Part A – Structure
- Part B – Fire Safety
- Part C – Contamination and damp
- Part D – Toxicity
- Part E – Sound
- Part F – Ventilation
- Part G – Hygiene
- Part H – Drainage
- Part J – Fuel
- Part K – On-site Safety
- Part L – Conservation of Fuel and Power
- Part M – Access
- Part N – Glazing
- Part O – Overheating
- Part P – Electrics
- Part S – Infrastructure for Charging Electric Vehicles

You will need to appoint a building inspector, who will ensure that your project meets building regulations. A building inspector will visit your project at various stages to ensure compliance.

You can find your local authority's **building** control department through your council website, which should give more information about charges and who to contact. You can also use an approved private Building Control company that can sign-off your work in the same way as your local council.

Do I need building regs for an extension?
If you are building an extension, then you will most likely need building regulations approval. Most extensions will need to meet a minimum set of technical standards.

The regulations you'll need to consider are likely to be:
- Energy performance (ensuring your build is insulated enough and has good airtightness so heat doesn't just leak out)
- Structural integrity as most extensions require foundations
- Protection against falls and unsafe walls
- Electric and gas safety as most extensions require new systems

- Fire protection which means ensuring there is safe passage from your home to a safe external area

How much is a building regulations application fee?
Most local authorities offer fee calculators on their websites. Their fees will depend on several factors including the type of work involved, size of the project and number of visits required. Private companies will negotiate their fees directly with you.

In England, Wales and Northern Ireland, once an application is lodged, work can commence on site within 48 hours.

Remember, on top of application fees, you will need to budget for plans and structural calculations, which can come in between £1,200-£4,000 plus, depending on the scale of your project.

What are the different types of building regulation applications?
Before any work can begin, you need to decide whether to make a Full Plans or a Building Notice application. With a Building Notice, it is possible to carry out the work without prior approval while a Full Plans application is where you submit plans and documents to be approved.

For most construction projects a Full Plans application is made to building control. If you choose a Full Plans application, you will know from the start that the working drawings have been checked and approved by the building inspector and that the plans fully comply with all of the Building Regulations.

Importantly, this means that any issues regarding non-compliance with the regulations can be thrashed out before building work actually starts. The application comprises of:

- A full description of the proposed works
- A set of technical drawings
- Structural engineer's calculations
- A location or 'block' plan

What is a building notice application for building regs?

With this method you're basically promising in advance that you'll comply with building regulations on site. This might be feasible for some small domestic alterations or a very simple home extension but it's harder for larger projects.

If your site inspections uncover stuff that contravenes the regulations while it's being built, such as the wrong type of insulation or too much glazing, work has to be stopped or re-constructed, which could prove disruptive, as well as costly.

Remember you still need to complete a form giving details of the building work together with a site plan (1:1250 or 1:12500 scale) showing the boundaries of site and drainage details.

You may also be asked to provide marked up sketch drawings (typically copies of those used for planning) together with structural engineer's calculations and energy performance details.

Do I need a structural engineer?

The plans required for building control are considerably more detailed than those submitted for planning and are often commissioned as an additional service.

Whether you choose to submit a Full Plans application or not, building control normally requires calculations from a qualified structural engineer who you can employ at the structural drawing stage.

What's more if you plan to make any structural alterations to your existing house, such as knocking down internal walls and openings, these may also need calculations.

Depending on the size and complexity of the project, and whether site visits are needed, engineer's fees typically range from around £400 for run-of-the-mill extensions to £3,000 plus for more complex houses.

How much do building regulation drawings cost?

For building regs drawings, expect to pay from around £700 for a single-storey extension, and around £1,200 for a two-storey extension, excluding additional charges for structural calculations, building control application fees and any party wall agreements.

Local Authority Building Control fees are published on local authority websites and typically cost around £1,000 for a new house but less than half that for an average extension or loft conversion.

In total, for the average new house you could expect to pay around £2,000, less if planning drawings have first been commissioned as there's a certain amount of overlap.

Large architectural practices can charge £75 or more per hour for this sort of work, and producing detailed technical drawings with a specification for a bespoke new house could set you back as much as £10,000.

How long do building regs take to come through?

For building control to process a Full Plans application the stipulated period of five weeks should be sufficient assuming there are no major issues.

Remember, you don't have to wait for 'plans approval' before starting work on site.

Who is responsible for building regulations approval?

You can choose to use:

- A local authority inspector from your local council and run through Local Authority Building Control (LABC)
- An approved inspector from a government-approved private building inspection company. Around 20% of all approvals are now handled privately, without recourse to the local authority

Approved inspectors are registered with the Construction Industry Council. They must re-register every five years to maintain high standards.

However, only an inspector from your local authority has powers of enforcement. An approved inspector must hand the project over to the local authority if there are problems with the project that cannot be resolved informally. There's very little difference in cost whether using an approved inspector or working directly with the local authority.

Builders and building regulations

While all good builders will know how to ensure their work meets building regulations standard, and the process for having their work signed off by Building Control, the onus of ensuring that building regulations are met lies with you as the homeowner. You can delegate this responsibility to your build team, but the legal responsibility remains with you.

The inspection process for building regs

Although work on a new build or extension may proceed before any formal approval, nothing can proceed beyond the inspection stages without the approval of the inspector.

Those inspection stages are:
- Excavations for foundations
- Foundation concrete
- Oversite
- Damp-proof course
- Foul water drains trenches open
- Surface water drains trenches open
- Occupation prior to completion (second fix)
- Completion

How do I get a completion certificate?

When the building is completed to the satisfaction of the inspector, a completion certificate will be issued. This is a vital document that must be retained alongside the written planning permission for use if you ever want to sell. It is also required in order to release final funds from lenders, obtain the warranty certification and in order to reclaim VAT (if applicable).

The completion certificate will not be available until all your certificates have been passed to the building control officer and a final site inspection has passed.

The relevant certificates vary from one project to another but usually include:

- Electrical safety
- SAP rating
- Air pressure test
- Boiler installation and hot water services
- Water efficiency calculations
- Security
- Fuel storage
- Remediation of contaminated land
- Chimneys and open flued appliances.

Selling a house without building regs

Any diligent solicitor will ensure that evidence of building regulations compliance such as a completion certificate is provided during a house purchase.

If you don't have a record of this for some reason, perhaps from work carried out by a previous owner, there are a few ways this can be tackled.

A regularisation certificate involves a retrospective application in which an inspector checks the build or alteration, but against the regulations that were in place at the time the work took place.

Indemnity insurance is also an option if the work has not been signed off, or paperwork is missing. This safeguards the property from legal action such as a building regulations enforcement from the local authority for the new owner.

However, this course of action does not offer the peace of mind that the work is safe, and with the property's structure and fire safety at risk, it's worth further exploration.

What is the competent person scheme?

In some instances, when an application to Building Control would be required, certain qualified fitters and installers are able to sign off the work and report it to the Local Authority. This includes trades such as window and door fitters, gas installers for the likes of new boilers and electricians.

****

Part 5

Party Wall Agreements Explained

> When you are contemplating works that may affect your neighbour, it is necessary to be aware of the requirements of the Party Wall Act 1996. One reason why the Party Wall Act is such a serious issue is because poorly executed structural alterations are a common cause of cracking and movement, and have even, on occasion, been implicated in the collapse of adjoining buildings.

The Party Wall Act 1996

All matters relating to Party Walls are covered by the above Act that came into force in 1997.

Party Wall Agreements ensure that your neighbour doesn't suffer loss or damage to their property due to your project and lets them limit disturbance by influencing working hours and access.

The Act and the agreement are in place to protect neighbouring properties and any disputes that may occur when work is carried out.

Party Wall defined

The Act recognises two main types of party wall.

Party wall type A

A wall is a "party wall" if it stands astride the boundary of land belonging to two (or more) different owners. Such a wall:

- is part of one building
- or separates two (or more) buildings
- or consists of a "party fence wall"

A wall is a **"party fence wall"** if it is not part of a building and stands astride the boundary line between lands of different owners and is used to separate those lands (for example a masonry garden wall). This does not include such things as wooden fences or hedges.

Party wall type B

A wall is also a "party wall" if it stands wholly on one owner's land but is used by two (or more) owners to separate their buildings. An example would be where one person has built the wall in the first place, and another has built their building up against it without constructing their own wall. Only the part of the wall that does the separating is "party" - sections on either side or above are not "party".

The Act also uses the expression "party structure". This is a wider term, which could be a wall or floor partition or other structure separating buildings or parts of buildings approached by separate staircases or entrances for example flats.

Walls that are not Party Walls:
These may include boundary walls (a fence wall/garden wall built wholly on one owner's land) and external walls (the wall of a building built up to but not astride the boundary)

When do I need a Party Wall Agreement?
The first step you must take before carrying out any physical construction onsite is to serve the adjoining owner(s) with a formal written notice, known as a Party Wall Agreement.

This normally needs to be actioned a couple of months before work begins (in some cases one month is sufficient, but the more notice you can provide the better).

Although this initial notice can be submitted on your behalf by appointing a solicitor or surveyor, it's often better to retain control at this preliminary stage.

The best approach is to first talk to your neighbours about your proposed extension to put their minds at rest before you or your surveyor issues the required notice. If your neighbours are tenants or leaseholders, you will also need to notify the freeholder or landlord.

Another good reason for making the initial approach yourself is that lawyers specialising in this area will generally advise adjoining owners not to give consent to a party wall notice, so that even where the neighbour is perfectly happy with your proposals, they may be persuaded to act in a way that seems uncooperative. This is because if the consenting neighbour subsequently needed to engage a surveyor to protect their position, they'd have to pay the surveyor's fee (if they don't consent, the person extending has to pay).

Is it a legal requirement to have a Party Wall Agreement?

If your proposed project includes works to a shared party wall or structure, you are required by law to serve notice on all affected neighbours at least two months before work starts. Below are some of the projects where you will most likely need a Party Wall Agreement before starting work:

1. Building foundations: if excavation is within a distance of 3m from the adjoining property, or where your new trench is deeper than their existing foundations.

2. Loft conversions: if you need to rest a new structural beam within the party wall when converting your loft.

3. Building an extension or a new wall: if you build right up to or astride the garden boundary wall or alter a party wall when building an extension.

4. Adding a basement: if you're digging deep foundations, are underpinning the party wall or need to cut into the party wall to insert beams.

5. Removing a chimney stack: if your chimney stack is shared with a neighbour as masonry you cut away will form part of the party wall.

Can you create a Party Wall Agreement yourself?

If your project is covered by the Act, a Party Wall Notice can be served to neighbours yourself or using a Party Wall Surveyor (more on which below). Perhaps surprisingly, it doesn't have to be an official legal document, although it must include certain key information along with drawings and details of the work.

The precise forms you need to issue will depend on the type of work you want to carry out. You can download appropriate Party Wall Notice forms online at www.gov.uk/government/publications/preventing-and-resolving-disputes-in-relation-to-party-walls/the-party-wall-etc-act-1996-explanatory-booklet

Another good site for free party wall forms is:

https://collier-stevens.co.uk/resources/party-wall-notice-templates

You give the Notice (with an explanatory booklet) and with a letter setting out your intentions, to all the owners of every neighbouring property affected. Remember to include all the key information, including:
- the date the Notice is served
- the date work will start
- all parties' names and addresses
- a description of the proposed work

If you don't do this, your Notice will be invalid.

Nature of the agreement
A verbal Party Wall Agreement will not be recognised as the official Party Wall Act has not been complied with. Consent or disapproval will need to be confirmed in writing

Cost of a party wall agreement
For a straightforward job outside London with an adjoining owner dissenting to the works, fees are likely to be in the

region of £1,000-2,000 plus VAT. However, you should note that party wall agreements can range from the above to up to £5,000 depending on the work involved to put them together. Fees will depend on the nature and complexity of the work being undertaken as well as the number of adjoining owners. And it is not always the case that the person instigating the work will pay all parties' fees. To get an accurate quote, consult a RICS accredited surveyor. It's also worth consulting them if you have had a Party Wall Notice served on you.

Is a Party Wall Notice mandatory?

If things turn sour with your neighbour and they suspect that the work being carried out will adversely affect their home, they can seek a court injunction to stop you from continuing.

If you haven't obeyed the Act and you cause major damage to your neighbour's property, the judge can award compensation for any loss or damage resulting from the works, including legal costs. An approved Notice is the only way to prevent this. If you are excavating near a neighbouring building then you need to give at least one month's notice of doing so. Once the neighbours have been served with the notice, they then have 14 days to respond on the acknowledgement form included with the original notice.

Once complete, present this, together with a copy of the Act and explanatory booklet, to your neighbour two months before starting.

Your neighbour will have 14 days to provide written approval or rejection.

- If they approve, your Notice will be valid for a year to complete work
- If they reject or do not respond within 14 days, then you're deemed to be in dispute

Neighbour objections

Should they disagree, or simply not bother to reply, the law deems this as non-consent and that a 'dispute' has arisen. The Act then provides a process for the dispute to be resolved. It's important to note that the adjoining owners cannot legally prevent the proposed building work from taking place because, for example, they don't like the idea of an extension next door, since this is a planning issue.

The only situations where they can actually prevent the construction work from proceeding is where an extension needs 'special foundations' such as piles.

In this example the neighbours could refuse outright, potentially scuppering the project. They are also allowed to refuse construction of what would become a new party wall if it's actually located on their garden boundary.

If approval is impossible, then you will have to assign an 'agreed surveyor' or two surveyors to prepare a Party Wall Award. This 'Award' covers:
- the work that can be carried out
- how the works will proceed
- timings
- measures for preventing damage
- the payment of surveyors' fees
- the current condition of both properties
- most importantly, costs payable to the adjoining owner if damage occurs

Assigning a Party Wall Surveyor
When a neighbour's consent can't be obtained the next step is normally to find a party wall surveyor. You're allowed to appoint a single 'agreed surveyor' to act jointly for both property owners because legally a party wall surveyor has to act as an impartial independent expert rather than as the agent for the client who appointed them.

In short, party wall surveyors help mitigate risk to all parties, and ensure that projects can progress without delay. If you correctly serve notice on your neighbours and damage occurs, any disputes over that damage will be dealt with by surveyors rather than at common law.

What if there is Still a Dispute?

If you're on good terms with your neighbours there's every chance they will accept what you're proposing. It goes without saying that the resulting expense, disruption, and possible contractual issues caused by having to stop work can be debilitating, hence the importance of complying with the legislation from the outset.

If your neighbour doesn't receive the required advance legal notification and then one fine day encounters builders excavating alongside their boundary, they can apply for an injunction to stop work. This can be done very quickly by lodging a claim in the County Court.

The injunction will then be served on the owner of the property being extended, ordering work on site to stop, with a date in court fixed so both sides can put their case.

Normally the errant building owner will acknowledge in court that they've failed to comply with the Party Wall Act and must give a written undertaking that they will henceforth comply, with the retrospective appointment of party wall surveyor(s) to issue an Award.

For full details about the Party Wall Act 1996 and also the processes involved (plus detailed diagrams) go to:

www.gov.uk/government/publications/preventing-and-resolving-disputes-in-relation-to-party-walls/the-party-wall-etc-act-1996-explanatory-booklet

Copies of useful (free) templates can also be found at www.collier-stevens.co.uk/resources/party-wall-notice-templates.

****

Part 6

When is planning permission not needed? Permitted developments and alterations.

> *Permitted Development Rights can help you avoid the need to apply for full planning permission if the size of your build meets the specific limits set out in the criteria. Porches, small extensions and loft conversions could all fall under Permitted Development. However, the criteria you have to meet is strict and it is easy to fall foul of the law.*

Homeowners and Permitted Development Rights

This implied consent of Permitted Development is granted in the form of General Development Planning Orders (GDPOs) which apply separately to England, Wales, Scotland and Northern Ireland.

There have been several new PD rights in England in recent years, including a significant change for extenders, which saw the introduction made back in September 2020 of a fast-track for two-storey extensions on homes.

Another change took effect in August 2020 that makes it easier to turn commercial premises into homes. A new class

MA ('Mercantile to Abode') now allows the conversion of any empty Class E commercial premises, such as offices, restaurants, shops and gyms into new homes without planning permission (see Chapter 2 Planning Use Classes).

What can I build or extend under permitted development?
The scope of Permitted Development rights is varied and covers both internal and external works, but there are strict design criteria that need to be adhered to. If your project falls outside of the set criteria, then it is likely you will need to submit a planning application. Some home improvements that you can make under Permitted Development include:
- Building a small rear extension within certain limitations, this includes both single storey extensions and double storey extensions
- Building a porch less than 3m2
- Changes of use, such as loft conversions, garage conversions and basement conversion
- Internal alterations, such as knocking down internal walls
- Installing microgeneration equipment such as solar panels (apart from wind turbines)
- Installing satellite dishes and erecting antenna
- Adding rooflights or dormer windows

What can't be built under Permitted Development?
Mansard loft conversion

Adding a box-like mansard type of loft conversion will more often than not exceed the size restrictions allowed under PD rights for loft conversions (see below) and would therefore need consent from the local authority.

Restrictions with Permitted Development

If you live in a flat or maisonette then PD Rights do not apply due to the impact that any alterations could have on neighbouring properties. If your house is located in a Designated Area, such as a National Park, Area of Outstanding Natural Beauty or Conservation Area then your Permitted Development rights may be restricted or removed under what is known as an Article 4 direction. This is where rights have been removed in the interest of maintaining the character of the local area. This could also be the case if your property is listed. Alternatively, if you're planning to self-build a replacement dwelling and your proposed new home is bigger than the existing house on site, then your Permitted Development rights are likely to be restricted or even removed on condition of granting planning permission. The Planning Portal www.planningportal.co.uk has more details concerning permitted development rights.

You should also double check with your local authority or get confirmation from a qualified surveyor that your proposed works are classed as Permitted Development before you begin.

If your project falls outside the scope of permitted development, you will need to apply for planning permission.

Prior approval

In England, PD rights allow larger single storey rear extensions subject to a 'Prior Approval' process of up to 8m on a detached house and up to 6m on any other house. The local planning authority must be notified of the details prior to development taking place. Details of the documents, drawings and fee (currently £96 in 2024) to be submitted will be available on your local authority website.

The LPA will write to the immediate neighbours (see Neighbourhood Consultation Scheme, below) and give them at least 21 days to decide if they wish to object. If there are no objections, then as long as an extension falls within the rules the LPA have to grant Prior Approval, the scheme can go ahead.

If there are objections the LPA will consider the impact of the proposal on the residential amenity of all adjacent neighbours and will either decide that the impact is acceptable and grant Prior Approval or take the view that the impact is not acceptable and refuse. There is a right of appeal against any refusal of a Prior Notification. For more information go to: www.gov.uk/guidance/appeals

The Neighbourhood Consultation Scheme

If you intend to build a large single-storey rear extension of between 4m up to 8m (for a detached house) or between 3m and up to 6m on any other house*, you can now typically do so under Permitted Development (PD). However, you will need to go through the Neighbour Consultation Scheme, which is a prior approval process for large extensions.

You must notify your local authority of your intention to build a large extension and they will then notify your adjoining neighbours and consult them about your planned extension. If your neighbours raise concerns, your local authority will decide whether your plans can go ahead.

Lawful Development Certificates

The difficult bit about Permitted Development is being absolutely certain you've interpreted the rules correctly. The way to be certain is to apply for what's called a Lawful Development Certificate.

You provide full details of what you intend to do, explaining how it complies with Permitted Development and submit this application to the council. It's not a planning application, it's a determination by them that what you want to do complies with the PD regulations. It takes about the same length of time as a planning application, but it's not discretionary based on planning officers' opinions or neighbour objections; it's a legal determination that you're doing something in accordance with the rules. It's a good way of being certain and when it comes to selling your house you can prove that it was legal. The cost of an LDC for proposed use or development is half the normal planning fee.

Permitted development categories

Permitted development rights do not remove requirements for permissions or consents under other regimes such as the building regulations and the Party Wall Act.

Householder permitted development rights are set out in the Town and Country Planning (General Permitted Development) (England) Order 2015 ("the Order") as amended. Part 1 of Schedule 2 to the Order sets out the permitted development rules concerning what enlargements, improvements, alterations and other additions a householder may make to their house and the area around it without the need for an application for planning permission.

The rules on permitted development, set out in Schedule 2 of the Order, are sub-divided into a series of Parts. Part 1 specifically deals with development within the curtilage of a house. Part 1 is then sub-divided into Classes covering various types of development:

Class A covers the enlargement, improvement or alterations to a house such as rear or side extensions as well as general alterations such as new windows and doors. There is a neighbour consultation scheme for larger rear extensions under Class A, paragraph A.1(g).

Class B covers additions or alterations to roofs which enlarge the house such as loft conversions involving dormer windows.

Class C covers other alterations to roofs such as re-roofing or the installation of roof lights/windows.

Class D covers the erection of a porch outside an external door.

Class E covers the provision of buildings and other development within the curtilage of the house.

Class F covers the provision of hard surfaces within the curtilage of the house such as driveways.

Class G covers the installation, alteration, or replacement of a chimney, flue or soil and vent pipe.

Class H covers the installation, alteration, or replacement of microwave antenna such as satellite dishes.

There are also other Parts of the Order that may be relevant to householders. For example, Part 2 covers matters such as erection or construction of gates, fences and walls, exterior painting, charging points for electric vehicles and CCTVs. Part 14 covers the installation of domestic microgeneration equipment such as solar panels.

Building Regs and Work Classed as PD

Building Regulations relate to the building work itself and not the permission to carry out the work, so your work must still comply with the stipulations of the Regs.

Neighbour objections

While a neighbour can object to any proposed changes to your home, the LPA will only be concerned with any objections that relate to material matters. To help avoid objections, keep your neighbours informed of your plans and listen to their concerns.

If any of your proposed works involve a party wall, you may need a party wall agreement. (See Part 5)

Construction not complying with Permitted Development

If, once an extension or outbuilding etc. is constructed, the LPA determines that the proposal does not comply with PD regulations then you may be faced with enforcement action, which would normally result in a request for a retrospective planning application. Should permission be refused there is a likelihood that any extensions or associated works would be required to be demolished. As such, confirmation in the form of the Lawful Development Certificate is highly recommended.

Planning permission for a home improvement project

In some areas, Permitted Development rights have been revoked, such as the ability to undertake a garage conversion under PD rights where on-road parking is an issue.

Another example is if you live in a designated area, such as a Conservation Area, or own a listed building. In these instances, PD rights often don't apply. Your property also has a limit to its Permitted Development rights, which don't reset when it changes ownership. That means if your home has already been extended, for example, its Permitted Development rights have already been allocated if you wanted to undertake a similar project in the future. Larger build projects, such as where you self-build, demolish and replace an existing building or create a large extension, will generally be subject to planning permission.

Extensions

If you want to extend your home then your project might well fall under PD rights. Under PD rights you can build an extension without planning permission as long as you meet certain criteria.

- You can extend a **detached** property by **8m to the rear** if it's a **single-storey** extension (6m for a semi or terraced house), or by **3m** if it's double
- A single-storey extension **can't be higher than 4m** on the ridge and the eaves, and ridge heights of any extension can't be higher than the existing property
- **Two-storey** extensions must not be closer than **7m to the rear** boundary
- Side extensions can only be single storey with a maximum height of 4m and a width no more than half of the original building
- Any new extension must be built in the same or similar material to the existing dwelling
- Extensions must not go forward of the building line of the original dwelling

- In designated areas (such as areas of outstanding natural beauty, conservation areas, etc.), side extensions require planning permission and all rear extensions must be single storey
- An extension must not result in more than half the garden being covered.

See the planningportal.co.uk for a full list of caveats.

If you don't need planning permission to extend your home and your project does fall under PD it is still wise to apply for a Lawful Development Certificate to state that the work done was lawful. This is especially useful if you go on to sell your home in the future.

Knocking down internal walls

It's unlikely that you'll need planning permission to knock down internal walls but there are exceptions, particularly if your home is listed or in a conservation area, so it's always worth asking your local authority It goes without saying that you need to know what you are doing here to avoid bringing down your house and while you won't need planning permission, you will need Building Regulations approval on structural elements and electrical works.

Replacing windows

Adding a bay window is classed as extensions, so will have to meet Building Regulations standards for extending, as well as fitting within your PD rights allocation.

You won't usually require planning permission to add a new window, or door, into your home. This counts for replacing windows and moving them too. However, if your building is listed, windows are one of the key areas where you may not be able to make a change, only replacing like for like, which could limit your options.

When it comes to inserting a new window on the upper storeys of the side elevation of your house, you'll require planning permission unless the windows are glazed with obscured glass to a standard of level 4 or 5 obscurity. They also must be a non-opening frame, unless 1.7m above the floor of the room the window is in.

There might also be instances where you may need to apply for planning permission for some of these works because your council has made an Article 4 Direction withdrawing Permitted Development Rights so again, always double check. For new or bigger windows or doors, you will need to follow Building Regulations guidance.

*

Converting a garage

An integral garage, or any building attached to the main house, to turn into a living space, it will probably fall under Permitted Developments.

However, if the garage was built after the house, you'll need to check with your local authority that this addition hasn't used your home's Permitted Development allocation. It's worth noting that converting a detached garage is more likely to need planning permission. It will also require a change of use application under Planning Permission.

Rooflights

Rooflights can be added under Permitted Development if they don't project more than 15cm from the slope of your roof. However, if the rooflights would extend forward of the roof plane on the elevation fronting a highway then they are not permitted and will require a formal planning permission application. It is worth noting that rooflights are not permitted on a dwelling which is located in a Conservation Area or an Area of Outstanding Natural Beauty.

Loft Conversion

A loft conversion adds extra space and value to a home without the need for planning consent. While there are limitations on the cubic content allowed under PD, generally, up to 40m³ is fine.

When it comes to additional headroom in the loft space, PD allows for the construction of dormer windows. However, they must not sit higher than the highest part of the existing roof or extend forward of the roof plane on the principal elevation.

Two Storey Extensions

Adding a two-storey extension under Permitted Development is a relatively new addition, designed to fast-track this sort of home improvement to create extra habitable space for homeowners. However, to qualify under PD rights, it must be at the rear of the dwelling (this includes adding a second storey onto an existing single storey part of the house).

The two-storey extension must also not exceed 3m in depth or be within 7m of the rear boundary. There are specific restrictions that apply to the design too, which can all be found on the Planning Portal.

New conservatory

Similar to single storey extensions, conservatories and orangeries fall under the same restrictions and can be added under PD. Conservatories stand-alone from most extensions however, as they can generally be built without Building Regulations sign off, if they're under 30m2 and have exterior grade doors separating them from the main house.

Sheds, garden office or outbuildings

There may be opportunity to build multiple outbuildings under PD, providing the total area covered by such buildings/enclosures does not exceed 50% of the total area of the curtilage. This 50% should take into account any extensions, but not the area covered by the main house.

- Outbuildings cannot sit forward of the principal elevation
- There are height restrictions depending on the type of roof (4m for dual pitch roofs, 3m for other roofs, and 2.5m when the building is within 2m of the boundary)
- Outbuildings may only be single storey, with the maximum eaves height remaining at 2.5m
- Outbuildings under PD cannot be used for residential accommodation, e.g. bedrooms or an annexe, but can be used to provide a place to work from home.

Converting two homes into one

Converting a pair of semi-detached houses or two flats into one property can usually be done under PD and can be a great way of generating extra space without having to move. The same rules do not apply if you are dividing a single property into two dwellings. For this you would need to apply for planning permission.

Adding another storey

In certain circumstances, a whole storey can be added to your house under PD rights. Full rules are available on the Planning Portal website, but some of the limitations include:
- One storey only can be added to single storey dwellings such as adding a second storey to a bungalow.
    - Two storey or more houses can add up to two storeys under Permitted Development.
    - The house cannot exceed 18 metres overall.
    - Each storey cannot add more than 3.5 metres to the height.
    - The storey must be on the principal part of the house and the roof pitch must be the same as it was before.

New porch
- As long as your new porch conforms with the criteria below, you don't need planning permission.
- No part of the porch can be taller than 3m
- It cannot be within 2m of any boundary adjacent to a highway

- The ground area (measured externally) does not exceed 3m².

Adding a fence or wall

Permitted Development facilitates the erection, construction, maintenance, improvement or alteration to a gate, fence, wall or other means of enclosure, providing such work stays within the following limitations:
- The height would not exceed 1m when adjacent to a highway
- The height would not exceed 2m for any other gate, fence etc
- Such development is not permitted under PD around a listed building

New garden decking

As long as the height falls below 300mm, garden decking and other similar structures can be built without planning permission, as long as certain criteria are met, including that decking platforms can't be over 30cm from the ground.

Swimming pools

Under your Permitted Development rights you can build a swimming pool within your garden, provided that the total area covered by the pool does not exceed 50% of the area of the garden curtilage.

Creating a new driveway

Permission to create a new driveway will depend on the classification of the road you are looking to create access from/to. Creating a new vehicular access onto an unclassified road can be done under PD, but you will need planning permission to create accesses onto classified roads. For a new access onto a classified road, you will need to ensure sufficient visibility when leaving the site, as well as enough turning space to allow you to enter and exit in a forward gear.

Creating parking spaces

Class F of the GPDO refers to the provision of hard surfaces, such as parking areas. These are permitted under PD providing that:

- any hard surface situated between the principal elevation of a dwelling and the highway, or any surface which would exceed 5m², is made of porous materials
- provision is made to direct run-off water from the surface into a permeable/porous area within the property curtilage and not onto the highway.

Changing cladding

Cladding (stone, pebble dash, render, timber, etc.) changes may fall under PD, but is not permitted under PD on any dwelling house located on Article 1(5) land (this includes special areas, like an AONB, National Park, World Heritage site or Conservation Area).

Adding solar panels to a roof

Solar panels can be added under PD, providing they do not protrude more than 200mm beyond the plane of the wall or roof, and that the highest part of the panel is not higher than the highest part of the roof (excluding the chimney).

Free-standing panels can also be developed but are limited in size and proximity to the boundary. Limitations will apply in Conservation Areas and on listed buildings.

Basements requiring planning permission

In a recent appeal decision, it was considered that basements could be PD under Class A of the General Permitted Development Order (GPDO). However, bear in mind that PD does not allow for engineering work.

*

Conversion of industrial/commercial buildings

It is possible to convert an industrial, commercial or agricultural building for residential use, without the need for planning permission. As is often the case, you will require approval for Listed Buildings and those in Conservation Areas. You will also need to follow the Prior Notification procedure if you are converting an agricultural building such as a barn.

Car charging ports

An electric vehicle charging point can be installed under PD rights, for areas being lawfully used for off-road parking. There are different restrictions on rights for wall-mounted chargers and charging stations with upstands, but neither have Permitted Development for listed buildings or sites classified as scheduled monuments.

When the charging point is no longer required for charging an electric car at home, these areas must be returned to their previous condition as soon as possible.

Outdoor security or lighting

While installing security systems, security lighting and general outdoor lighting is not subject to planning control, nor requires PD rights, there are some considerations to keep in mind when specifying for your home. Lighting should be installed ensuring that beams are not pointing directly at neighbours' windows, while automatic PIR or timer lights should be set up in a way not to cause nuisance, including being triggered by people passing your property on the street. Failure to consider these could land you in court with a neighbour if considered to be negligent or causing a nuisance.

Installing a Ground Source Heat Pump
If you want to install a ground source heat pump then this will usually be considered as permitted development, which means you won't need to file for planning permission. Contact your council to check on local requirements if you live in a listed building or a conservation area.

Installing an air source heat pump
Again, as with ground source heat pumps, you don't have to apply for planning permission to install an air source heat pump but there are strict conditions to adhere to that are listed on the Planning Portal website. An air source heat pump should be installed and commissioned by an accredited Microgeneration Certification scheme (MCS) installer.

Work on Drains

Repairing drains or making minor amends won't usually require planning permission but you should always double check with your local council in case drains are shared with neighbours.

If you are extending your home and the new building will go over a drain then you will need to get a Build Over Agreement with a CCTV drainage survey to evaluate what's there, where the pipes run and how it could be altered. It might be that your extension plans will have to alter to accommodate the drains. Drainage rules are outlined in Approved Document H.

It must be noted also that Scotland, Wales and Northern Ireland each benefit from their own version of these rules, so it is always best to check with the relevant planning authority.

****

Part 7

Contesting Proposed Developments

> *In theory, when your local council's planning department receives an application for development, they are supposed to notify all of those within a given radius of the planning site. However, this is in theory. It will very much depend on the council. This will include neighbours and local businesses in more densely populated areas.*

In reality however, this will come down to the discretion of your council's planning officer(s). This regularly leads to situations where many people who believe they should be informed do not get a letter or any notice.

Finding Out about Planned Developments.

One way of keeping up to date with planning applications in your area is to frequent your local Council's website. Councils are required to keep records of applications that have been received. In many cases you will be able to see what other people have already said about them and download all the details of the applications yourself. If you do not have access to the internet, you should be able to request copies of applications to inspect by visiting your Local Council's Planning Department. In some cases, these records are also available in your local library.

Making a Planning Objection to the council

In order to make an objection to a planned development you must write to your local council's planning department. You can do so either by post or in some cases email. Always better to do both. Many planning departments also have a dedicated website.

When writing a letter, it is important to reference the planning application number (shown on the Council's initial letter/email to you or on the Council's website). The letter should be sent to the address of the department.

In general, the more people that submit an objection, the greater the likelihood that the council will take it seriously.

It is, in the first instance, best not to organize a petition; councils seldom pay these any attention and it will be unlikely to bolster your case. Also, the council will respond more favourably to disputes that clearly originated in the own words of their writers. Councils are required to request comments to a planned development within a fixed time frame. This is typically within 1 day of notice. In practice, however, they will take into account representations received before final decisions are made on the application.

Grounds for disputing a planning application

When writing your application, it is important to understand what actually constitutes a legitimate argument against a planned development. There exists a broad list of reasons you can put forward as the basis of an objection.

Negative/adverse visual impact of the development – of particular concern is the impact a proposal will have on local landscape and points of interest

Issues with the Design proposed – this includes:
- Designs that are out of scale or "character"
- Detailing and materials that are poorly matched with the area
- Ignoring local design (determined by comparison and any guidelines)

Negative effects on community – due to:
- Noise
- Disturbance

- Overlooking & loss of privacy
- Nuisance
- Shading/ loss of daylight

Be sure to provide examples of the above in your letter. Planning officers do not look kindly at what they consider to be unfounded claims.

Over development – This is especially relevant if changes will be out of character in the area.

Conservation Areas & Listed Buildings – Any impact that the planned development may have on a Conservation Area or Listed Buildings.

What Council will not accept as grounds for an objection
The following arguments should never be used as grounds for an objection.
- The applicant's ethnic origin, religious beliefs, or sexual orientation
- Impact on property valuation in the aera of the planning site
- Boundary or other unresolved civil disputes

- The applicant's personal circumstances or other private matters
- Claims about the behaviour or reputation of the applicant or their representatives
- Hearsay about other unspecified work or alternative uses of the application site (unless covered by the application)
- Matters relating to prior negative experiences such as previous nuisances caused by the applicant

Many people object to planning on the grounds that the effect of construction (i.e. dust, noise, nuisance caused by construction traffic etc.) is causing a major impact on themselves or their community. This is not a planning consideration as such, in all but extreme cases this is unlikely to be considered by the planning authority.

When you send your objection letter, be sure to ask your post office for a certificate of posting. This is a must. In general, decisions on whether to grant planning permission are made by officers who were delegated the responsibility to do so under powers specific to your local council. These planning officers will be charged with considering whether objections submitted are worthy grounds to reject an application.

In particularly complex or controversial cases, a planning committee will be convened to make the decision instead. If this is going to take place, then you will be able to attend and, in some cases, will be permitted to make your case. The process itself varies based on the council. You should be able to find out more information by visiting the planning department of your local council's website.

****

Part 8

Farms-Planning Permission and Permitted Development Rights for Farms

When you need Planning permission

Farms are covered by the same planning regulations as other types of property. Some planning rules include special conditions for agricultural buildings and land. You need planning permission if:

- you want to change how you use your land or buildings from farming to something else
- you want to build a house on the land

You will also usually need planning permission if you are applying for a grant to fund a project that needs a building or other development.

When you do not need it

You do not need planning permission:

- for farming operations

- to use buildings already on your land for farming purposes
- to change the inside of a building, or make small alterations to the outside - for example, installing an alarm box
- if there are permitted development rights
- Before starting work on the project, always check with:
- your local planning authority in England and Wales
- your local planning authority in Scotland
- your local area planning office in Northern Ireland

Permitted development

As we have seen in the previous chapter, permitted development rights (PDRs) are useful procedures that make certain types of development quicker, easier and cheaper. They allow landowners to build, extend, develop, convert, excavate or carry out engineering work on certain sites without going through the full planning permission process, and some have been designed specifically for agricultural buildings. These rights are set out in The Town and Country Planning (General Permitted Development) Order 2015.

Permitted development means that if your farm is 5 hectares or more, you have the right to:

- erect, extend or alter a building

Farms-Planning Permission and Permitted Developments

- carry out excavations and engineering operations needed for agricultural purposes, though you may still require approval for certain details of the development
- The types of permitted development include:
- temporary uses of land
- agricultural buildings below a certain size
- forestry buildings
- caravan sites and related buildings in some circumstances

Check with your local planning authority (or local area planning office in Northern Ireland) before making use of permitted development rights to make sure your development will not need planning permission.

What types of agricultural PDRs are there?
Class A

Permitted development related to agricultural buildings (including machinery and grain stores) and engineering/excavation rights on units of 5ha or more of agricultural land is known as Part 6, Class A development.

This allows you to erect, extend or alter a building, including excavation or engineering operations, all of which must be reasonably necessary for the purposes of agriculture within the unit.

Typically, this includes hard surfacing for field access and farm tracks and the building of machinery stores and grain stores, as long as they meet certain conditions governing siting, size and, in some cases, materials.

There must be no development:
- On a separate parcel of land that is less than 1ha and which is part of the agricultural unit
- Where dwellings are involved
- Where something is not for agricultural use
- Where the ground area of the building or development is more than 1,000sq m (except for fencing)
- Where any part of the development is within 25m of a metalled part of a trunk road or classified road
- Of a building (or involving work to a building) intended for or used by livestock, slurry or sewage sludge housing and within 400m of the curtilage of a dwelling. The curtilage usually means the physical boundary of the land surrounding a dwelling. If the works are within 400m of buildings within an agricultural unit (or a dwelling or other building on another agricultural unit), they are excluded from this restriction.

- Anything involving excavations or engineering operations connected with fish farming on certain protected land types (for example, National Parks).

Height restrictions also apply where the work is within 3km of the perimeter of an aerodrome.

There are other conditions, too, mainly concerning removal of minerals from the site and waste materials being brought on to a site.

Class O

Farmers with buildings used as offices can change them to houses under Class O.

This can be carried out anywhere as long as it is not: a listed building, safety hazard zone, military explosives storage area, an ancient monument, or where the local authority has obtained an article four preventing this type of conversion. It must have been an office on or before 29 March 2013.

Class Q

Class Q allows for the change of use of an agricultural building to a house. In 2018, the regulations were amended to allow for up to five dwellings and up to 865sq m floor space to be converted. The building must have been in agricultural use on 20 March 2013 and the development cannot extend beyond its existing external dimensions.

Class Q cannot be used for a listed building or one within a conservation area, National Park, Area of Outstanding Natural Beauty, World Heritage Site or a site of special scientific interest.

Class R

Class R permits the change of use of agricultural buildings to a flexible commercial use of a retail unit, restaurant or café, office, commercial storage/distribution use, hotel, or a range of leisure uses, such as a concert hall or gymnasium.

On any one farm, the conversion should not exceed 500sq m. **Class R** applies to buildings in agricultural use on 3 July 2012 that are not listed or part of a scheduled ancient monument, safety hazard area or military explosives storage area.

Class S

Class S permits the change of use of agricultural buildings to a state-funded school or registered nursery.

On any one farm, the conversion should not exceed 500sq m. Class S applies to buildings in agricultural use on 20 March

2013 that are not listed or part of a scheduled ancient monument, safety hazard area, military explosives storage area or site of special scientific interest. Development is not permitted by Class S if the site is occupied under an agricultural tenancy, unless the express consent of both the landlord and the tenant has been obtained.

How do I use permitted development rights?
You must submit an application form to your local planning authority for confirmation of whether prior approval is needed for the siting, design and external appearance of a building, work or excavation.

This application currently costs £96 (2024). You should include a written description of the proposed development, materials and a plan showing the site.

The local authority then has 28 days to confirm in writing whether prior approval is needed or not. Where it isn't needed, work can go ahead as long as it's in line with the proposal submitted. Where it is needed, the local authority may ask for more details or changes to siting, design and materials. A notice containing specified information must also be publicly displayed at the site. If it is to go ahead, the development must be started within five years or the approval lapses.

****

Glossary of terms

Access – How you would get in and out of a site from the highway.

Agricultural permitted development – Things which can be done on agricultural land without needing formal planning permission.

Agriculture / Agricultural land – Land used for agriculture, and for farming trade or business purposes. It does not include houses or gardens, or land used for fish farming.

Appeal / appellant – An applicant for planning permission can appeal against a decision (usually a refusal of permission). Appeals can also be made if a planning authority does not decide an application in a given time, and for other reasons. The person who makes an appeal is the appellant. Appeals are decided by the Planning Inspectorate.

Appearance – How something looks, or its form. In planning, it is usually the appearance of the outside of buildings which matters.

Applicant -The person who signs and submits the planning application forms. An agent can submit applications for other people.

Area of Outstanding Natural Beauty – An area identified in law as nationally important because of its outstanding landscape value.

Building regulations – Building regulations set standards for the design and construction of buildings. They are designed to keep people in and around buildings safe and healthy. They also deal with energy saving measures and provide disabled access in buildings.

Certificate of Lawfulness of a Proposed Use or Development – People can apply to find out whether a proposed development is lawful in planning terms. If it is, the Certificate is issued by a local planning authority, meaning that the proposed development will not need planning permission.

Change of use – Changing the use of a building, or plot of land, from one use class to another use class is seen as development. It therefore needs planning permission.

Committee – A group of people who make decisions on planning matters. The committee is part the local planning authority and made up of elected councillors (or members).

Committee report / report to committee – Before an application goes to planning committee, the officer dealing with the application writes a report to explain the issues. It usually describes any public response to the application, provides an analysis of the issues, and makes a recommendation to approve or refuse. Conditions, or reasons for refusal, are also usually suggested.

Community / communities – A general term used to describe the people who live together in a neighbourhood, village, commune, hamlet or centre of population. Communities can also be based around a religion, a set of interests, a profession, etc.

Community Involvement Scheme – Sets out the local planning authority's approach and a timetable for involving local communities in preparing Local Development Plans.

Conditions – Attached to a planning permission, conditions control how different parts of a development should be carried out. Conditions can be used to control many things – building materials, landscaping and access are just a few examples.

Consent – Permission

Conservation – Protecting something from harm or damage and improving it if possible. In planning, conservation is usually about a special landscape or environment, or it might be a building or part of town.

Conservation areas – Conservation areas are parts of villages or towns which are special because of their architecture or history. Local planning authorities designate conservation areas to protect or improve their special qualities. A higher standard of design is expected in the area, and any pulling down of buildings or cutting of mature trees is controlled. =

Consultant – A planning consultant is a trained planner who works for people and companies who can afford to pay for expert help and advice. Consultants have experience of the planning system and use it in many ways, for example, to help get planning permission or to appeal against a refusal.

Consult / consultation – Asking people or organisations what they think about something. Comments are usually asked for on a particular matter (such as a planning application), or a set of issues, or a draft document (such as public participation in preparing a plan). Consultation can be formal or informal. It can involve everybody in an area, or a small selection of people or groups.

Contamination / contaminated land – Land that has been polluted or harmed in some way, making it unfit for safe development. Development can only happen after it has been cleaned up, or decontaminated.

Core strategy – Part of a development plan. The core strategy sets out in very general terms how an area will develop in the future. It gives the plan a central framework, which allows more detailed planning policies to be prepared for specific areas and topics.

Deemed consent – Does not need a formal planning application, and consent is not needed.

Design – Indicates the look and 'feel' of the building, both inside and outside. It includes the materials used, how energy efficient something is, and landscaping.

Determine – A local planning authority determines a planning application when it reaches a decision on whether to grant planning permission. It also determines whether a proposed development will need planning permission.

Development – Defined as 'the carrying out of building, engineering, mining or other operations, in, on, over or under land, or the making of any material change in the use of any building or other land.' Development control – The process by which a local planning authority receives, considers the merits of, and determines planning applications.

Development control decisions are usually based on the development plan and other material considerations. Often, an authority will have a separate development control section or department.

Development plan – The document which uses words and maps to set out the local planning authority's policies and proposals for future development in its planning area. Usually looking fifteen years forward, it contains policies for specific sites and for different types of development. Development plans include Unitary Development Plans, Structure Plans and Local Plans.

Enforcement / enforcement notice – A local planning authority uses its enforcement powers to make sure all the terms and conditions of a planning decision are carried out. Enforcement is also used to control development which has not got a planning permission, but which needs it. An enforcement notice sets out what needs to be done to put something right, or to control an activity which has not got planning permission.

Environmental Impact Assessment – Some types of development, usually bigger schemes, need an Environmental Impact Assessment. Applicants will need to prepare an Environmental Statement and include it with the planning application. The statement considers the likely impacts of the development on the environment. It also looks at how the impact can be reduced. It is used to help decide the planning application.

Environmental Statement – Looks at the likely environmental impact of a proposed development. It contains the findings of the Environmental Impact Assessment, and often a lot of supporting background information. The statement should contain a description of the development, measures to be taken to avoid harming the environment, and the main likely effects on the environment. The statement should also describe alternatives looked at, and reasons for choosing the final proposal. A layperson's summary is also provided.

Full application – A planning application with all the details of a development proposal. Sometimes referred to as a detailed application, it can be given full planning permission. There are no matters which are reserved for discussion and approval at a later date.

(see 'outline permission').

Inspector – An independent, experienced planner who works for the Planning Inspectorate. Looks carefully at detailed planning issues which are debated during examination of a development plan, or at a public inquiry into a specific proposal. Inspectors also decide appeals.

Judicial Review – Where the High Court looks at whether a decision made by a planning authority is reasonable. Some planning decisions are tested by a Judicial Review.

Landscaping / landscaping proposals – Includes plants, trees, paths and structures. A landscaping proposal should be prepared for areas of land which will not be built on. Often forming part of a planning application, it might include garden layouts, walls and fencing, trees and planting areas, and 'hard' road and pavement surfaces.

Listed building consent – Needed for the demolition or part-demolition of a listed building. Also needed to alter or extend a listed building, where the work would affect the building's character or special interest. Also needed for any work to other buildings in the grounds of a listed building.

Listed building – A building which is protected from development because of its special historic interest or architecture. Local planning authorities should hold a list of the listed buildings in its area, which the public can see.

Local Development Plan – Often called a 'LDP', it will is the statutory development plan for a local planning authority area. It should include a vision and a broad strategy, as well as policies for different areas and types of development. It will identify land suitable for new development and set out proposals for key areas of change and protection. Policies and development land will be shown on a map base, called the Proposals Map.

Local planning authority – The local authority or council that is responsible for preparing plans and for making planning decisions. The planning authorities also deal with waste and minerals matters.

Local Plan – An old-style development plan which sets out detailed policies and proposals for the development and use of land. In some authorities, local plans are still used to guide decisions on planning applications.

Objection – Words, usually written, which give reasons for objecting to a development proposal or policy. People can make an objection to a planning application, or to something which is contained in a draft development plan or policy, or at appeal.

Outline application – Planning applications can be submitted in outline to find out if the principle of a development on a site is acceptable. If a proposal gets outline planning permission, details of the development will need to be approved at a later date. Usually only used for larger applications.

Permitted development / permitted development rights – There are certain types of development which do not need planning permission. These include small works and things which will not have much of an effect on other people. The General Permitted Development Order sets out those things which can be done without needing to apply for planning permission.

Planning committee – The committee of the local planning authority which makes decisions on planning applications and development plan policies.

Planning Inspector – An experienced planner. The Inspector makes independent planning decisions and considers appeal cases and tests the 'soundness' of development plans at examination. They also make decisions at public inquiries into larger proposals. Inspectors write reports considering all the planning evidence and decide cases.

Planning permission – Formal approval from a local planning authority that a proposed development can go ahead. It is often granted with conditions. Usually, the development needs to be started within a given time of permission being granted. Planning Permission can be full, or outline.

Public consultation – Informing members of the public about a planning application, or about future plans for an area. Usually involves asking people to make comments within a set time. Comments received are taken into account before a decision is made.

Public Inquiry – A formal hearing held by a planning inspector into a planning matter. It might be into a local development plan, or an appeal. Members of the public can attend public inquiries as observers and can also be invited to comment on an issue.

Recommendation – A planning officer makes a recommendation to the planning committee. It is usually set out towards the end of the committee report on the planning application. The recommendation is the professional opinion of the planning officer, but the committee do not have to take the recommended decision. Recommendations are usually to refuse, to approve, or to defer.

Registered – Once a planning application is received by a local planning authority, it is checked to make sure it includes all the information needed. It is then registered.

Representation – Comments which are submitted to a local planning authority. They can either be in support of something, or they can object to something. Representations are usually made in connection with a planning application, or a proposed policy in a development plan for the area.

Reserved matters – Things to do with a proposed development which will need to be decided at a later date. For instance, an outline application for housing on a site is approved – however, more detail is needed on the design of each house, the materials to be used, and landscaping. These are reserved matters, because they still need to be approved.

Stop Notice – A legal notice served by the local planning authority which aims to make somebody stop a development or an activity. Used as part of enforcement powers.

Strategic Environmental Assessment – Development plans and certain other types of plan need to be assessed to see how they will affect the environment. The assessment is a process which happens as part of plan-making. It has a number of key stages – preparing an environmental report, looking at alternatives, carrying out consultations, and showing that the assessment has had an effect on the final plan. It is usually combined with Sustainability Appraisal, which considers social and economic effects, as well as environmental effects.

Sui generis – A Latin word which describes a land use, or building which is not in a Use Class. Examples of land uses which are sui generis include theatres, launderettes, car showrooms and petrol filling stations.

Sustainable development – Looking after the world by using its resources in a sensible way. Or, 'development that meets the needs of the present without compromising the ability of future generations to meet their own needs'. The planning system is important for sustainable development – it can bring about more sustainable ways of living and working. It can also encourage new types of development which use less energy

Unitary Development Plan – Often called a 'UDP', a plan covering the whole local planning authority area. It replaces old-style structure and local plans. It contains policies for the whole plan area, and identifies land for different kinds of development. Once formally adopted, it becomes the development plan for their areas.

Use Class – Planning law puts the different ways of using land and buildings into different Use Classes. To change the use of a piece of land, or a building from one use to another use within the same Use Class does not need planning permission. However, a change of use from one Use Class to another will usually need planning permission.

Utility company – A company which provides a product or a service which is used by the public. Examples include water, electricity, gas and telephone utility companies.

Visual amenity – The contribution made by the look of a place to how the public enjoy it. An area with high visual amenity is pleasing and attractive to the eye

Written representations – A written statement setting out comments, or an argument for or against something. The simplest way of submitting an appeal to the Planning Department.

****

Useful information and websites

Architects

Contact architects in your area. There are many sites online but the below two sites are particularly useful.

www.myhomeextension.co.uk/architectural-design
www.mybuilder.com/post-a-job/architectural-services

Surveyors

www.localsurveyorsdirect.co.uk/planning-permission-applications-consultancy

The Planning Portal

www.planningportal.co.uk
www.planningportal.co.uk/wales

The (English and Welsh) Planning Portal is an online application system based in Bristol. They are not part of any council and do not have a planning department so cannot offer planning advice. Therefore, if you need planning advice or are unsure of which form to submit please contact you local councils planning department.

Building control planning portal

www.planningportal.co.uk/applications/building-control

Scotland and Northern Ireland have their own planning portals.

Scottish equivalent

www.edevelopment.scot/eDevelopmentClient/CustomPages/login.aspx

Northern Ireland portal

www.northernirelandplanningegister.planningsystem.ni.gov.uk

Guide to the Planning System

www.gov.uk/government/publications/plain-english-guide-to-the-planning-system/plain-english-guide-to-the-planning-system

A very useful and clear guide to all aspects of the planning system.

Register of planning decisions

www.gov.uk/search-register-planning-decisions

Royal Town Planning Institute

www.rtpi.org.uk/need-planning-advice/planning-aid-england/online-advice-service/

Which? Planning advice

www.which.co.uk/reviews/extensions/article/extension-planning/building-regulations-and-planning-permission

****

Index

Adding another storey, 3, 130

Affordable housing, 17

Agricultural Land Declaration, 3, 57, 60

Airbnb, 3, 43

Appealing against a planning decision, 3, 76

Applications made under the Planning (Hazardous Substances) Act 1990, 55

Applying for costs, 77

Approved private Building Control company, 93

Areas of Natural Beauty, 46

Builders and building regulations, 98

Building Act 1984, 85

Building regulations, 3, 85, 89, 90, 152

Building Safety Act 2022, 86

Car charging ports, 3, 134

Cavity wall insulation, 90

Certificate of Lawful Use, 3, 42

Changes to the description of the development, 70

Commencement Notices, 25

Community Infrastructure Levy ("CIL"), 28

Competent person scheme, 3, 101
Conservation Areas, 46, 75, 133, 134, 140
Conservatories, 128
Contesting Proposed Developments, 137
Converting a garage, 3, 127
Creating a new driveway, 3, 132
Creating parking spaces, 3, 132

Delay in validation of an application, 70
Department for Levelling Up, Housing and Communities., 21
Design and Access Statement, 3, 57, 63, 64, 65, 67
Enforcement, 23, 24, 28, 78, 98, 101, 123, 156, 162
Enforcement notices, 78
Enforcing planning breaches, 3, 23
Environmental enhancement, 18
Environmental Impact Assessment, 3, 57, 69, 73, 81, 156, 157

Farms, 3, 143

Green Belt reform, 3, 16
Green space improvement, 18
Grounds for disputing a planning application, 3, 139

Heat-producing appliances, 90
Home improvement project, 3, 123

Infrastructure Levy ("IL"), 28
Internal walls, 3, 96, 116, 125

John Leslie Finney v Welsh Ministers & Carmarthenshire County Council, Energiekontor (Uk) Limited, 27
Judicial review, 3, 22

Landscaping, 50, 158
Lawful Development Certificates, 3, 119
Levelling-up and Regeneration Act 2023, 3, 15, 24, 25
Listed building consent, 3, 53, 62, 63, 64, 65, 66, 67, 74, 77
Local Government Ombudsman, 3, 24
Local information requirements, 3, 69
Local Planning Authority, 20
Location plan, 57
Loft Conversion, 3, 127

Making a planning application on paper, 3, 55
Mansard loft conversion, 117

National Development Management Policies ("NDMP"),, 26
National Development Management Policies (NDMPs), 3, 17
National information requirements, 3, 56
National Planning Policy Framework, 19, 69
Neighbourhood plans, 19

Northern Ireland, 3, 13, 19, 30, 31, 32, 45, 46, 81, 87, 94, 115, 136, 144, 145

Obtaining Planning Permission, 45
Outbuildings, 129
Outline planning application, 3, 49
Outline planning applications details, 3, 67
Ownership Certificate, 3, 57, 60

Party Wall Agreements, 3, 12, 103
Permitted development categories, 3, 120
Permitted Development Rights, 3, 87, 115, 126
Planning breach, 23
Planning Use Classes, 3, 35, 116
Plans and drawings, 3, 56, 57
Reserved matters, 3, 49, 68, 162
Rooflights, 3, 127

Scale, 50
Scotland, 3, 13, 19, 30, 45, 46, 81, 86, 87, 115, 136, 144
Strategic reviews, 18
Swimming pools, 3, 131

The Crown, 53
The Department for Business, Energy & Industrial Strategy (BEIS), 53

The Levelling-up and Regeneration Act 2023,, 15

The Neighbourhood Consultation Scheme, 3, 119

The Party Wall Act 1996, 3, 103

The planning register, 80

The Town and Country Planning (Use Classes) Order 1987 (as amended), 35

Town and Country Planning Act 1990 ("TCPA"), 27

Tree Preservation Order, 48

Two Storey Extensions, 3, 128

Types of planning application, 3, 47

Wales, 3, 13, 19, 28, 29, 30, 31, 45, 46, 81, 85, 87, 88, 94, 115, 136, 144

Work on Drains, 3, 136

****

Case study-Design and Build and the Planning Process
Building a house-brief history and drawings

Paul and Jayne Marshall:

We first got involved in self-build in 1999 and got the idea initially through friends who were looking for properties. They found that the cost of a house at that time was far too expensive and decided to explore other avenues.

We were also in the same boat and discussed the problem with a builder friend of ours, who offered to build a house for us, subject to finding a plot of land, which is always the main consideration. We found a plot in our home village, a house with an orchard, both on the market but later split into two plots, of which we bought one, which had been granted outline planning permission. The initial price was £40,000. We approached the estate agent as it had been on the market for three months and offered £25,000 for the plot. This was rejected and Jayne contacted the owner who met us on site. She stated that she had never received the revised offer. We offered £27,000, which was accepted. This was our very first self-build and we have never looked back.!

After receiving working drawings from the architect, we initially drew up and presented our preferred designs and they then came back with several alternatives. We looked at new build show homes in order to get ideas for interiors, such as fitted wardrobes and also went online to look at different lighting set ups. We looked at different kitchen designs and, finally, we decided that we would go for under-floor heating, which makes sure that the heat is more evenly distributed, each room having a thermostat, and also eliminates the need for radiators on the ground floor, although they would be needed on the first floor.

Overall, a lot of thought, time and effort went into the final design. We wanted to ensure that we maintained control of the process and have maximum input at the outset. This is particularly recommended for all first-time self-builders who lack experience. Hindsight is a wonderful thing although it can be expensive when the house has finally been constructed!

See below the initial (proposed) design creations for our current self-build. These show the ground and first floor of the dorma bungalow and also the whole layout.

Planning permission

The most important point when it comes to obtaining planning permission, whether outline or full, is that you need to use an architect. As seen in the previous chapter on planning permission, they will let you know what they would charge for taking on the project and steer you through the design process, along with making the planning application. They will also deal with building control issues. In addition, they can arrange for a topographical survey and also deal with the local utilities, such as water authorities who need to provide clearance before you can build.

There are many issues when seeking to obtain planning permission to construct a property. The most important ones, in our case, were those of access, due to the proximity of the main road, and traffic coming out onto that road and also privacy issues, light issues and so on. We found that the delegated planning powers given to staff in the planning department were enough to get through most hurdles but, with one of our projects we encountered complex issues and the application eventually went to the full committee.

Below, we have included the drawings put together by our architect, Paul Gaughan, Building Consultants, which enabled us to get the proposed construction through planning and which provided working drawings for our builder and assisted in the design process.

See overleaf for detailed drawings produced for Paul and Jayne Marshall's self-build by their architect.

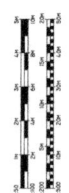
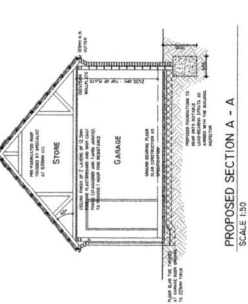

PROPOSED SECTION A - A
SCALE 1:50

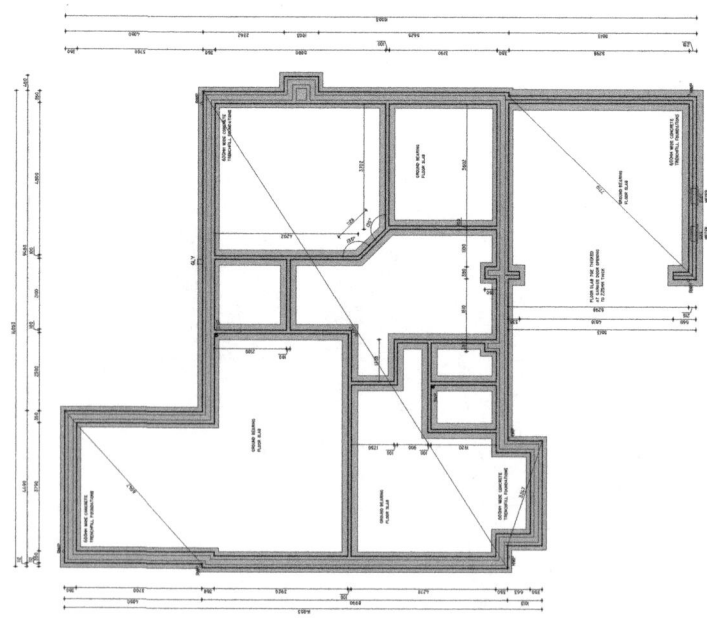

PROPOSED FOUNDATION LAYOUT
SCALE 1:50

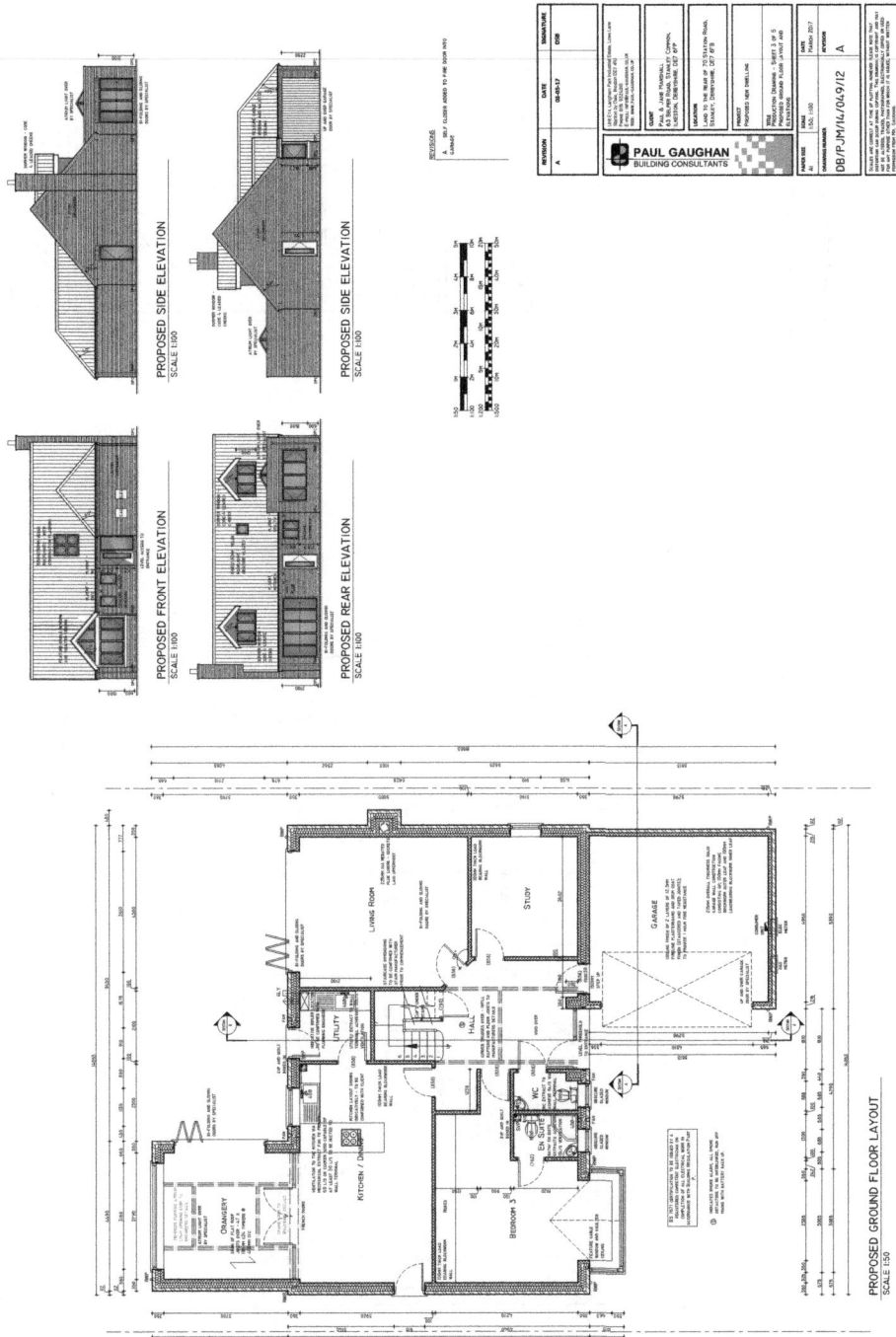

REVISIONS

REVISION	DATE	SIGNATURE

PAUL GAUGHAN
BUILDING CONSULTANTS

Unit E14, Langham Park Industrial Estate, Lows Lane
Stanton by Dale, Ilkeston DE7 4RJ
PHONE 0115 9324010
E-MAIL: INFO@PAUL-GAUGHAN.CO.UK
WEB: WWW.PAUL-GAUGHAN.CO.UK

CLIENT
PAUL & JANE MARSHALL
63 BELPER ROAD, STANLEY COMMON,
ILKESTON, DERBYSHIRE, DE7 6FP

LOCATION
LAND TO THE REAR OF 70 STATION ROAD,
STANLEY, DERBYSHIRE, DE7 6FB

PROJECT
PROPOSED NEW DWELLING

TITLE
PRODUCTION DRAWING - SHEET 4 OF 5
PROPOSED FIRST FLOOR LAYOUT

PAPER SIZE	SCALE	DATE
A1	1:50	MARCH 2017

DRAWING NUMBER	REVISION
DB/PJM/14/049/13	.

SCALES ARE CORRECT AT TIME OF PLOTTING HOWEVER PLEASE NOTE THAT DISTORTION CAN OCCUR DURING COPYING. THIS DRAWING IS COPYRIGHT AND MAY NOT BE ALTERED, TRACED, PHOTOGRAPHED, ELECTRONICALLY COPIED OR USED FOR ANY PURPOSE OTHER THAN FOR WHICH IT IS ISSUED, WITHOUT WRITTEN PERMISSION FROM MR. GAUGHAN.
CHECK ALL DIMENSIONS ON SITE.
HATCHING IS A REPRESENTATION OF MATERIALS ONLY.

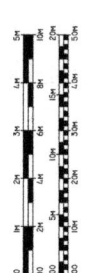

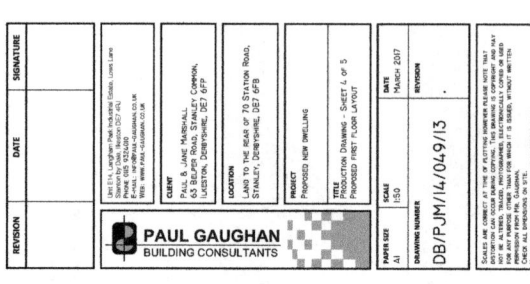

PROPOSED FIRST FLOOR LAYOUT
SCALE 1:50

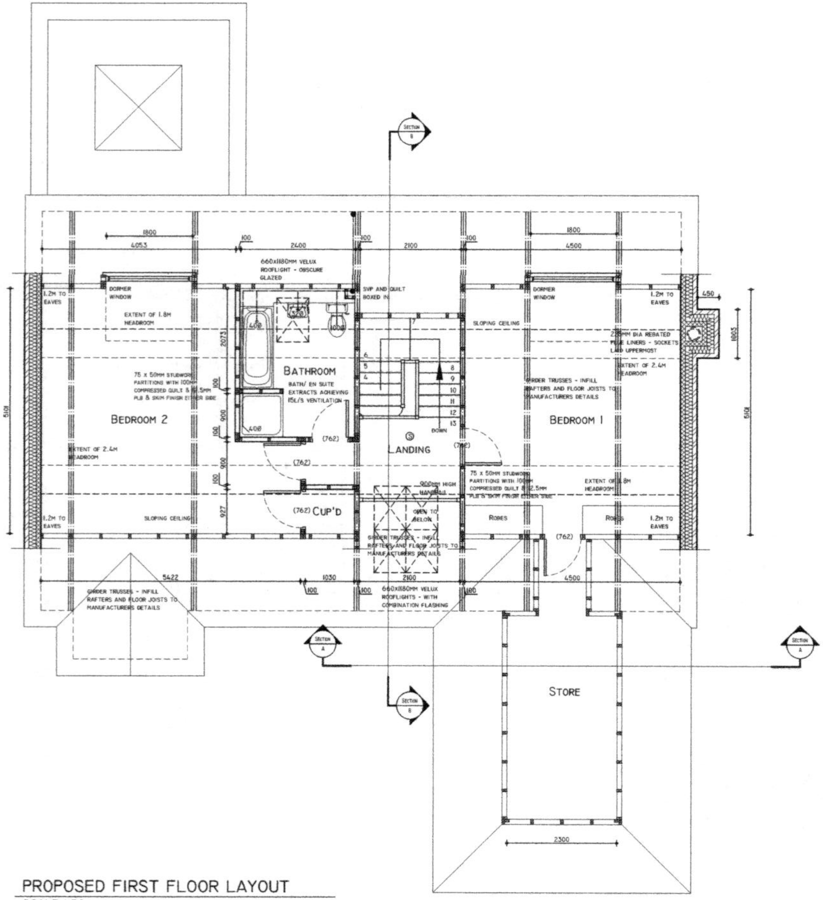

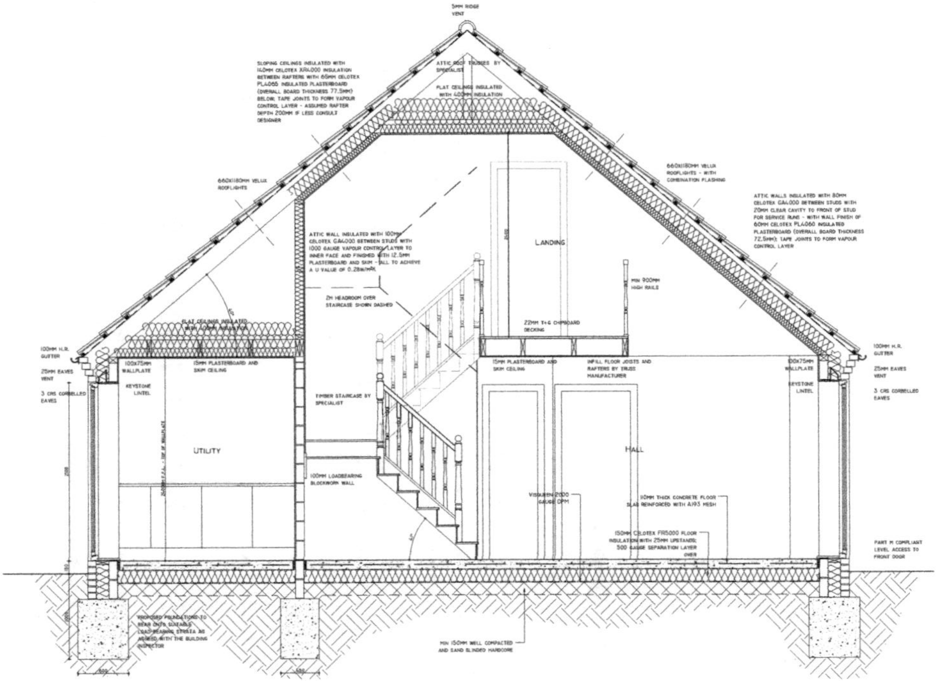

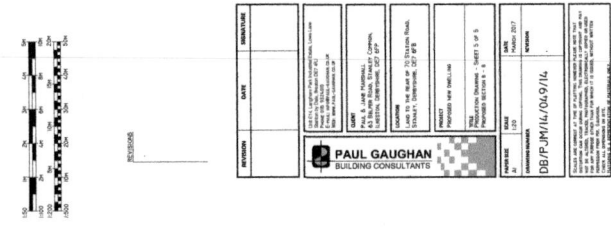

www.erewash.gov.uk **EREWASH**

Resources Directorate, Planning & Regeneration
Town Hall Ilkeston
Derbyshire DE7 5RP
Switchboard: 0115 907 2244

Mr Paul Gaughan
Unit E14, Langham Park
Lows Lane
Stanton By Dale
Derbyshire
DE7 4RJ

TOWN AND COUNTRY PLANNING ACT 1990

NOTICE OF DECISION

Part 1: Applicant Details

Applicant: **MR MARSHALL**

Application Ref: **ERE/0615/0023**

Proposal: **ERECTION OF A DETACHED THREE BEDROOM CHALET BUNGALOW WITH ROOMS IN THE ROOF SPACE**

Site Address: **LAND TO REAR OF, 68 & 70 STATION ROAD, STANLEY, DERBYSHIRE, DE7 6FB**

Part 2: Decision

Erewash Borough Council in pursuance of powers under the above mentioned Act hereby

GRANT PERMISSION

for the development in accordance with the application, subject to compliance with the condition(s) imposed (in Part 3 below), and the subsequent approval of all matters referred to in the conditions:

Part 3: Condition(s)

1. The development shall be begun before the expiration of three years from the date of this permission.

Reason
To comply with the requirements of Section 91 of the Town and Country Planning Act 1990.

2. This permission relates to drawings: Site Location Plan (1:1250) and Drw Nos. DB/PJM/14/049/03 Revision A (Proposed Site Block Plan) & DB/PJM/14/049/02 (Proposed Floor Layouts and Elevations), all validated on the 11th June 2015. Any variation to the approved drawings may need the approval of the local planning authority.

Reason
For the avoidance of doubt as to what is approved.

3. Prior to any other works commencing, the entire site frontage shall be cleared, and maintained thereafter clear, of any obstruction exceeding 1m in height (600mm for vegetation) relative to the road level for a distance of 2.4m from the nearside carriageway edge in order to maximise the visibility available to drivers emerging onto the highway.

Reason
In the interests of highway safety.

4. The proposed dwelling shall not be occupied until space has been provided within the application site in accordance with the revised application drawings for the parking of residents' vehicles, laid out, surfaced and maintained throughout the life of the development free from any impediment to its designated use.

Reason
In the interests of highway safety.

5. Notwithstanding the provisions of Part 2, Schedule 2 of the Town and Country Planning (General Permitted Development) (England) Order 2015 (or any Order revoking and re-enacting that Order), no gates or other barriers shall be erected across the entire frontage of the application site unless planning permission has first been granted by the local planning authority.

Reason
To allow for easy access and egress in the interests of highway safety.

6. The construction of the dwelling shall not commence until samples of the proposed materials to be used in the external construction of the development, including areas of hardsurfacing, have been submitted to, and approved in writing by the Local Planning Authority and the development shall only be undertaken in accordance with the materials so approved and shall be retained as such thereafter.

Reason
To ensure a satisfactory standard of external appearance.

7. The proposed dwelling shall not be occupied until a detailed scheme for the boundary treatment of the site, including position, design and materials, and to include all boundaries or divisions within the site, has been submitted to and approved in writing by the local planning authority. The approved scheme shall be completed before the dwelling is first occupied or such other timetable as may first have been agreed in writing with the local planning authority.

Reason
To preserve the amenities of the occupants of nearby properties and in the interests of the visual amenity of the area.

8a) The development shall not commence until a scheme to identify and control any environmental risk is developed and undertaken. This will include a desk top study (Preliminary Risk Assessment / Phase I Investigation) and, if indicated by the desk top study, an intrusive investigation (Generic Risk Assessment/ Phase II Investigation). The desk top study and then the scope of the intrusive investigation must be approved in writing by the local planning authority before commencement. In reaching its decision to approve such proposals the local planning authority will have regard to currently pertaining government guidance as set out in the CLR series of documents (particularly CLR 11) issued by DEFRA or any subsequent guidance which replaces it.

b) A written method statement detailing the remediation requirements to deal with any environmental risks associated with this site shall be submitted to and approved in writing by the local planning authority prior to commencement of the remedial works. The method statement should also include details of all works to be undertaken, proposed remediation objectives and remediation criteria, timetable of works and site management procedures. All requirements shall be implemented according to the schedule of works indicated on the Method Statement and completed to the satisfaction of the local planning authority prior to the development being brought into use. No deviation shall be made from this scheme without the express written agreement of the local planning authority.

c) If, during the development, any contamination is identified that has not been considered previously, then, other than to make the area safe or prevent environmental harm, no further work shall be carried out in the contaminated area until additional remediation proposals for this material have been submitted to and approved in writing by the local planning authority. These proposals would normally involve an investigation and an appropriate level of risk assessment. Any approved proposals shall thereafter form part of the Remediation Method Statement.

d) Prior to the development first being brought into use a verification report must be submitted to the Local planning authority demonstrating that the works have been carried out. The report shall provide verification that the remediation works have been carried out in accordance with the approved Method Statement. The development should not be brought into use until the verification report has been submitted to and approved in writing by the local planning authority.

e) In the event that it is proposed to import soil onto site in connection with the development the proposed soil shall be sampled at source such that a representative sample is obtained and analysed in a laboratory that is accredited under the MCERTS Chemical testing of Soil Scheme or another approved scheme the results of which shall be submitted to the local planning authority for consideration. Only the soil approved in writing by the local planning authority shall be used on site.

Reason
To ensure that risks from land contamination to the future users of the land and neighbouring land are minimised, together with those to controlled waters, property and ecological systems, and to ensure that the development can be carried out safely without unacceptable risks to workers, neighbours and other offsite receptors.

9. No development shall take place until the scheme of intrusive site investigations as detailed in the submitted Coal Mining Risk Assessment dated May 2015 has been undertaken. A report detailing the findings arising from the site investigation shall be submitted to the Local Planning Authority before any development commences. If any land instability issues are found resulting from, for example, past mining activity during the site investigation, a report specifying the measures to be taken to remediate the site to render it suitable for the development hereby permitted shall be submitted to and approved in writing by the Local Planning Authority. The site shall be remediated in accordance with the approved measures before development begins.

Reason
To ensure that risks from land instability and mining related hazards to the future users of the land and neighbouring land are minimised, and to ensure that the development can be carried out safely without unacceptable risks to workers, neighbours and the general public.

10. The hours of working on the construction of the development, and deliveries to/collection from the development site shall only take place between the hours of 7.30am and 6.00pm on Monday to Friday; 8.00am and 1.00pm on Saturday with no working taking place on Sundays, Bank and Public Holidays.

Reason
In the interests of residential amenity.

Part 4: Positive and proactive statement

There were no problems for which the Local Planning Authority had to seek a solution in relation to this application.

Part 5: Notes to applicant

1. Pursuant to Sections 149 and 151 of the Highways Act 1980, steps shall be taken to ensure that mud or other extraneous material is not carried out of the site and deposited on the public highway. Should such deposits occur, it is the applicant's responsibility to ensure that all reasonable steps (e.g. street sweeping) are taken to maintain the roads in the vicinity of the site to a satisfactory level of cleanliness.

2. Due to the location of the site within a residential area the applicant should take all reasonably practicable steps to minimise noise and dust nuisance that may arise from activities on site. The applicant is also advised that material arising from the clearance of vegetation should not be burnt on site in order to prevent smoke nuisance being caused to neighbouring properties.

Date: 14 August 2015   Signed _____
                           Steve Birkinshaw
                           Head of Planning & Regeneration

ATTENTION IS CALLED TO THE NOTES BELOW

Discharge of Conditions fees:
http://www.planningportal.gov.uk/uploads/english_application_fees.pdf

Appeals to the Secretary of State

- If you are aggrieved by the decision of your local planning authority to refuse permission for the proposed development or to grant it subject to conditions, then you can appeal to the Secretary of State under section 78 of the Town and Country Planning Act 1990.

- If you want to appeal against your local planning authority's decision then you must do so within 6 months of the date of this notice.

- Appeals must be made using a form which you can get from the Secretary of State at Temple Quay House, 2 The Square, Temple Quay, Bristol BS1 6PN (Tel: 0303 444 5000) or online at www.planningportal.gov.uk/planning/appeals

- The Secretary of State can allow a longer period for giving notice of an appeal but will not normally be prepared to use this power unless there are special circumstances which excuse the delay in giving notice of appeal.

- The Secretary of State need not consider an appeal if it seems to the Secretary of State that the local planning authority could not have granted planning permission for the proposed development or could not have granted it without the conditions they imposed, having regard to the statutory requirements, to the provisions of any development order and to any directions given under a development order.

DELEGATED ITEM REPORT

APPLICATION REFERENCE: ERE/0615/0023

ADDRESS:
Land to Rear of
68 & 70 Station Road
Stanley
Derbyshire

DESCRIPTION

ERECTION OF A DETACHED THREE BEDROOM CHALET BUNGALOW WITH ROOMS IN THE ROOF SPACE

PROPOSALS

Full planning permission is sought to erect a detached three bedroom chalet bungalow with rooms in the roof space at the rear of Nos. 68 and 70 Station Road, Stanley. The main body of the proposed dwelling will measure approximately 14m (w) by 9m (d) with a height of 6.4m (2.5m high to the eaves). An attached garage will project 5.5m from the front elevation and a single storey orangery will project 4.05m from the rear elevation. The rooms in the roof space will be served by two rear dormers and front & rear roof lights. The main body of the proposed dwelling will be sited approximately 4m from the rear elevation of No.70 Station Road, 5m from the boundary with No.64 Station Road, 1.1m from the boundary with No.92 Station Road and 13m from the rear boundary.

The proposed dwelling will provide approx. four off-street parking spaces and will be accessed via a shared driveway to the eastern side of Nos. 68 & 70.

SITE AND SURROUNDINGS

The site is located within the village envelope and currently forms part of the rear garden to No.70 Station Road. The area contains a mix of house types in a range of orientations. The site, other than the shared driveway, is sited approximately 21m away from the back edge of the public highway. Boundary treatment consists of approx 1.6m – 1.8m high fencing plus planting to the sides and rear boundaries.

The application site falls within a referral area in relation to historic coal mining activity in the area.

RELEVANT SITE HISTORY

0684/0056 - Erection of detached bungalow - Approved

0205/0033 - Erection of detached bungalow - Refused on highway grounds and backland development - Appeal Dismissed

0213/0026 - Erection of detached bungalow – Refused on highway grounds (intensification of use of a substandard access, restricted visibility & potential danger to other highway users)

POLICY CONTEXT

National Policy

National Planning Policy Framework (NPPF)

Erewash Core Strategy

Policy A: Presumption in Favour of Sustainable Development
Policy 2: The Spatial Strategy
Policy 8: Housing Size, Mix and Choice
Policy 10: Design and Enhancing Local Identity

Erewash Saved Policies

H3: Village Housing Development
H12: Quality and Design
DC1: Backland and Tandem development

Supplementary Planning Documents

Erewash Borough Supplementary Planning Document (SPD) 2006: Design

CONSULTATIONS

Ward Councillors – No representations received.

Stanley and Stanley Common Parish Council – No objection in principle to the proposed bungalow and backland siting subject to neighbour consultation. The proposed access arrangement for Nos.68/70 however appears to remove the current open fronted access arrangement and forwards entrance and exit vehicle access for these existing properties and the Parish Council would consider the application proposals an undesirable and retrograde step given the nearby sharp bend in the highway and actual egress visibility conditions existing here.

DCC Highways – Comments as follows:
- The Highways Authority has been involved in pre-application discussions with the agent. Consistently raised concerns over achievable visibility and intensification of use of existing access but unlikely to recommend refusal for an additional dwelling should the former access to the western side be re-opened under permitted development subject to the sites frontage being cleared to maximise visibility and space for parking and manoeuvring being provided. Whilst this would not be ideal, the eastern access would continue to serve two dwellings.
- Concerns over the applicant's/agents methodology/reasoning used in arriving at the achievable visibility from the existing access.
- Mitigation to offset traffic impact of proposed development.
- Both accesses fall below modern criteria in terms of emerging visibility.
- The eastern access will be shared by No.70 and the proposed dwelling so will provide access for two dwellings.
- Applicant is able to offer improvements by securing a parallel sightline 2.4m back from the nearside carriageway edge across the entire site frontage together with

2m x 2m x 45 degree pedestrian intervisibility splays on either side (where achievable).
- No highways objections subject to conditions requiring a unilateral undertaking to be entered into to ensure that the western vehicular access and parking area be utilised by residents of the existing property and maintained throughout the life of the development, space to be provided for construction workers, vehicles, storage of plant and materials etc, clearance of the site frontage to maximise visibility, and removal of permitted development rights for gates or other barriers across the site frontage.

In addition to the above, the Council sought further clarification on the above comments to which further comments were subsequently received to clarify that the Highways Authority is not saying that the residents must use the western access/parking, but that it should be provided and maintained available.

Severn Trent Water – No representations received.

Coal Authority – Part of the application site falls within the defined Development High Risk Area. Concur with the recommendations of the Coal Mining Risk Assessment Report. No objection subject to a condition requiring intrusive site investigations to be carried out prior to development.

EBC Environmental Health – No objection subject to conditions concerning hours of construction, dust, site clearance and contaminated land.

REPRESENTATIONS

Adjoining neighbours were notified of the proposals and a site notice was erected. Representations received from the occupiers of Nos. 64 & 92 Station Road. Comments as follows:

No.64 Station Road:
- The site location map shows a brook that runs along the bottom of the site but this is not specified on the application form.
- Proposal previously refused twice on the grounds of unsuitable site access.
- The road is not a slow speed or lightly trafficked rural lane as outlined in the submitted transport report.
- There have recently been a few accidents nearby on the road.
- The proposal seems to be trying to shoehorn a large 3 bed, garage and two storey bungalow into a back garden of an already extended property which is unsuitable for such a development.
- The two storey nature of the proposed property may affect the privacy of any neighbouring properties on all sides.

No.92 Station Road:
- No objection to the principle of the development but have a number of objections to the current proposal.
- The plan does not indicate the existence of our sewer which runs across the land in question. We fear this development poses a serious risk to our sewer.
- The proposed property is extremely close to our garden boundary and the very high roof line would block light to our fruit & veg garden and would feel oppressive.

- Feel that the proposed property could be more centrally located on what is a large plot of land.
- Dispute the evidence in the transportation plan as the traffic flow and parking surveys were carried out well outside peak time hours. In reality the traffic flow and level of on-street parking is far higher than assumed in the report.
- The plans show a turning area for the new property but none for No.70.
- We would not be against a new building on the plot if it had a lower roof line, is further away from our boundary, and does not compromise our sewer.

ASSESSMENT

The main issues for consideration in the determination of this application are considered to be:

- The principle of the development;
- The design of the proposal and impact on the character of the area;
- The impact of the proposed dwellings on the amenity of residents;
- Highway safety;
- Other matters.

The principle of the development

The site is located within the village envelope and is close to local services and public transport. The site is currently surplus garden land and subject to the details of the application it is the type of site that the NPPF supports as being appropriate for development. In addition the Saved Policy H3 supports this type of small-scale housing development within the village of Stanley subject to matters of design, access and location. Accordingly the principle of the development is considered to be acceptable and appropriate in this instance and accords with the NPPF, Core Strategy Policies A and 2, and Policy H3 of the Saved Policies, subject to consideration of the following detailed matters.

The design of the proposal and impact on the character of the area

The siting of the proposed dwelling to the rear of Nos. 68 & 70 ensures that whilst it will be visible from Station Road, it will not have a street presence. Its divergence from the character of the area which is of period two and three storey dwellings, with a front to back orientation generally with a road frontage, is contrary to the general character of the area. However there are examples of historical backland development within the area, and as such the design and character of the proposed dwelling is not considered to be so alien as to warrant a refusal of the planning application. It is therefore considered that the proposal will not present significant harm to the character of the area or the street scene as a result of its backland location. Whilst a planning application in 2005 was refused and the appeal dismissed on the grounds of backland development it is considered that since that time the general presumption of planning policy has shifted such that there is a presumption in favour of sustainable development and the Council heavily relies on this type of site coming forward to uplift its housing provision. The development is on balance considered to be acceptable in relation to Saved Policy DC1 as whilst it does not reflect the general pattern of development it does not result in significant harm to the character of the area with limited visibility within the street scene available. The amenity space provided for the dwelling is considered to be of sufficient size and will provide an acceptable level of amenity for future occupiers. The proposal is therefore considered to comply with the policy requirements relating to design and local identity/character within Policy 10 of the Core Strategy and Policy H12 of the Saved Policies.

The impact of the proposal on nearby residents

The proposed dwelling will be within the 45-degree line of vision from the rear windows of Nos. 64 & 92 Station Road and directly to the rear of Nos. 68 & 70 Station Road. However, this would be at a distance of some 9m from No.64, 15m from No.92, and 10m from Nos. 68 & 70 at its closest point (15m to the main body of the proposed dwelling). Whilst there would be some loss of outlook experienced to these properties, the resultant harm to the occupiers' amenity is not considered sufficient enough to warrant refusal of the application on this ground, particularly when noting the distance to the rear windows of these properties. The proposed dwelling will be set in 6m from the boundary with No.64 to the western side. This, together with the separation distance to that property (9m), is considered sufficient to ensure no undue impact on the residential amenity of the occupants of No.64 through loss of outlook, loss of light or overbearing impact. The proposed dwelling will be set in 1.1m from the boundary with No.92 to the eastern side and approx. 15m from the rear elevation of this property. Concerns have been expressed by the occupiers of No.92 that the building would be overbearing and result in a loss of light to the rear garden. When noting the distance to the rear elevation of that property it is considered that the proposal would not be unduly overbearing. The siting of the proposed dwelling adjacent to the boundary will create an element of overshadowing to the rear garden area of No.92, however any loss of light will be contained towards the rear of the garden and well away from the existing dwelling and as a result the resultant harm to the occupiers amenity through overshadowing / loss of light is not considered so severe as to warrant refusal of the application. Similarly it is not considered that the proposed dwelling would present significant harm to No.96 Station Road which is sited on the opposite side of the rear garden of No.92. It is therefore considered that the proposed dwelling will not cause significant detriment to the amenity enjoyed by the occupiers of neighbouring properties through a loss of outlook, loss of light or overbearing impact.

The proposed ground floor side windows to the western side elevation are not considered to present unreasonable privacy concerns through overlooking given that they will be set well away from the side boundary with No.64 whilst no windows are proposed to the eastern side elevation. The ground floor front windows and the front facing roof lights are not considered to present unreasonable privacy concerns to neighbouring properties to both sides or the front. The separation distance between the proposed rear dormer windows within the roof, and the rear elevations of neighbouring properties to the rear, will be approx. 25m. The proposed dormer windows will also be sited approx. 13m-16m from the angled rear boundary of the site. The separation distances proposed are considered sufficient to prevent significant harm through overshadowing or overbearing impact whilst the proposed dormer windows are not considered to result in a significant loss of privacy through a degree of overlooking above that ordinarily expected in a residential environment, particularly when noting the proposed separation distances. Similarly, it is not considered that the proposed rear windows would result in a significant loss of privacy to neighbouring properties to both sides.

Access to the site is obtained from Station Road alongside Nos. 68 & 70 and adjacent to some of the principal windows to both of these dwellings. Of concern is the impact of this drive adjacent to these neighbouring property windows which has the potential to result in undue noise and disturbance to the current and future occupiers of these dwellings. However as the proposal serves only one additional dwelling it is considered that these movements would be limited and whilst there will be some additional traffic movements again it is considered that this will not amount to significant detriment to the occupiers of Nos. 68 & 70 Station Road.

Accordingly, the proposal is considered to comply with Policy 10 of the Core Strategy and Policy H12 of the Saved Policies which seek to ensure that the amenity of neighbouring occupiers is not adversely affected.

Highway safety

The proposed development will be accessed via the existing vehicular to the eastern side of Nos. 68 & 70. DCC Highways Authority have raised concerns over the applicants methodology/reasoning used in arriving at the achieved visibility from the existing access to Station Road, but have noted that the proposal offers improvements to existing visibility and that the re-use of the vehicle access / parking space to the western side of Nos. 68 & 70 would offset the resultant intensification of the eastern access created by the proposed dwelling. They have therefore raised no objection subject to a unilateral undertaking being entered into to ensure that the western vehicular access and parking area be maintained throughout the life of the development, and subject to conditions requiring the access, visibility splays, and parking spaces to be provided in accordance with the application drawings. In response to this a site visit confirmed that the vehicular access / parking space to the western side is in-situ and would appear to be an established access (albeit one that has previously been fenced off but now re-opened) that benefits from an established dropped kerb. Whilst the previous application was refused on highway safety grounds, it is noted that the western access did not form part of the considerations as at that time the access was fenced off from the highway. However, since this time the fence has been replaced with a gate and the access has been re-opened. It is therefore considered reasonable to consider its presence and availability for use by the occupiers of No.68 when assessing the highways impacts of the current application, notwithstanding its location outside of the application site, and in this regard the Highways Authority have not objected to the current proposal for the intensification of the use of the eastern access subject to the western access being provided and maintained available. Given that the western access is in-situ and available for use, it is considered that the application should be assessed on its merits at the time of the application. In this regard it is not considered necessary to enter into a unilateral undertaking to ensure that this is provided. In addition to the above it is considered that sufficient off-street parking will be provided by the proposed development whilst sufficient space will also be available for the parking of vehicles to the side of No.70. The concerns raised by neighbours and the Parish Council in relation to parking provision, access, visibility, turning area and the details contained in the transportation report are duly noted. However, it is noted that national planning policy, in the form of the NPPF, now specifies that developments should only be refused on highway safety grounds where the impacts of the development are severe. As the Highways Authority have not identified severe harm from these proposals, it is concluded that the concerns over highway access do not constitute justified reasons for refusal.

Other matters

The comments of the Council's Environmental Health Officers relating to contaminated land and the control over the hours of construction, noise and dust, can be embodied in conditions or notes to the applicant, as can the comments of the Coal Authority in relation to intrusive site investigations.

The comments received from the occupiers of Nos. 64 & 92 in relation to the brook and potential impact on the sewer are noted. The impact of the development on any sewers that pass beneath the site is not a material planning consideration and such details will be assessed separately as part of the building regulations application. It is considered that the narrow watercourse shown on the site location plan will be unaffected by the proposed development due to its location approximately 9m away from the closest point of the proposed dwelling.

Conclusion

The proposed development of the site for a three bedroom chalet bungalow is within a sustainable location; the plot is of an appropriate size; the scale and design of the dwellings are considered acceptable; the development would not have an adverse impact on the residential amenity of neighbouring properties and the proposal is not considered to result in severe detriment to highway safety. Accordingly the development is considered to be acceptable.

RECOMMENDATION APPROVE

CONDITIONS & REASONS

1. The development shall be begun before the expiration of three years from the date of this permission.

Reason
To comply with the requirements of Section 91 of the Town and Country Planning Act 1990.

2. This permission relates to drawings: Site Location Plan (1:1250) and Drw Nos. DB/PJM/14/049/03 Revision A (Proposed Site Block Plan) & DB/PJM/14/049/02 (Proposed Floor Layouts and Elevations), all validated on the 11th June 2015. Any variation to the approved drawings may need the approval of the local planning authority.

Reason
For the avoidance of doubt as to what is approved.

3. Prior to any other works commencing, the entire site frontage shall be cleared, and maintained thereafter clear, of any obstruction exceeding 1m in height (600mm for vegetation) relative to the road level for a distance of 2.4m from the nearside carriageway edge in order to maximise the visibility available to drivers emerging onto the highway.

Reason
In the interests of highway safety.

4. The proposed dwelling shall not be occupied until space has been provided within the application site in accordance with the revised application drawings for the parking of residents' vehicles, laid out, surfaced and maintained throughout the life of the development free from any impediment to its designated use.

Reason
In the interests of highway safety.

5. Notwithstanding the provisions of Part 2, Schedule 2 of the Town and Country Planning (General Permitted Development) (England) Order 2015 (or any Order revoking and re-enacting that Order), no gates or other barriers shall be erected across the entire frontage of the application site unless planning permission has first been granted by the local planning authority.

Reason
To allow for easy access and egress in the interests of highway safety.

6. The construction of the dwelling shall not commence until samples of the proposed materials to be used in the external construction of the development, including areas of hardsurfacing, have been submitted to, and approved in writing by the Local Planning Authority and the development shall only be undertaken in accordance with the materials so approved and shall be retained as such thereafter.

Reason
To ensure a satisfactory standard of external appearance.

7. The proposed dwelling shall not be occupied until a detailed scheme for the boundary treatment of the site, including position, design and materials, and to include all boundaries or divisions within the site, has been submitted to and approved in writing by the local planning authority. The approved scheme shall be completed before the dwelling is first occupied or such other timetable as may first have been agreed in writing with the local planning authority.

Reason
To preserve the amenities of the occupants of nearby properties and in the interests of the visual amenity of the area.

8a) The development shall not commence until a scheme to identify and control any environmental risk is developed and undertaken. This will include a desk top study (Preliminary Risk Assessment / Phase I Investigation) and, if indicated by the desk top study, an intrusive investigation (Generic Risk Assessment/ Phase II Investigation). The desk top study and then the scope of the intrusive investigation must be approved in writing by the local planning authority before commencement. In reaching its decision to approve such proposals the local planning authority will have regard to currently pertaining government guidance as set out in the CLR series of documents (particularly CLR 11) issued by DEFRA or any subsequent guidance which replaces it.
b) A written method statement detailing the remediation requirements to deal with any environmental risks associated with this site shall be submitted to and approved in writing by the local planning authority prior to commencement of the remedial works. The method statement should also include details of all works to be undertaken, proposed remediation objectives and remediation criteria, timetable of works and site management procedures. All requirements shall be implemented according to the schedule of works indicated on the Method Statement and completed to the satisfaction of the local planning authority prior to the development being brought into use. No deviation shall be made from this scheme without the express written agreement of the local planning authority.
c) If, during the development, any contamination is identified that has not been considered previously, then, other than to make the area safe or prevent environmental

harm, no further work shall be carried out in the contaminated area until additional remediation proposals for this material have been submitted to and approved in writing by the local planning authority. These proposals would normally involve an investigation and an appropriate level of risk assessment. Any approved proposals shall thereafter form part of the Remediation Method Statement.

d) Prior to the development first being brought into use a verification report must be submitted to the Local planning authority demonstrating that the works have been carried out. The report shall provide verification that the remediation works have been carried out in accordance with the approved Method Statement. The development should not be brought into use until the verification report has been submitted to and approved in writing by the local planning authority.

e) In the event that it is proposed to import soil onto site in connection with the development the proposed soil shall be sampled at source such that a representative sample is obtained and analysed in a laboratory that is accredited under the MCERTS Chemical testing of Soil Scheme or another approved scheme the results of which shall be submitted to the local planning authority for consideration. Only the soil approved in writing by the local planning authority shall be used on site.

Reason
To ensure that risks from land contamination to the future users of the land and neighbouring land are minimised, together with those to controlled waters, property and ecological systems, and to ensure that the development can be carried out safely without unacceptable risks to workers, neighbours and other offsite receptors.

9. No development shall take place until the scheme of intrusive site investigations as detailed in the submitted Coal Mining Risk Assessment dated May 2015 has been undertaken. A report detailing the findings arising from the site investigation shall be submitted to the Local Planning Authority before any development commences. If any land instability issues are found resulting from, for example, past mining activity during the site investigation, a report specifying the measures to be taken to remediate the site to render it suitable for the development hereby permitted shall be submitted to and approved in writing by the Local Planning Authority. The site shall be remediated in accordance with the approved measures before development begins.

Reason
To ensure that risks from land instability and mining related hazards to the future users of the land and neighbouring land are minimised, and to ensure that the development can be carried out safely without unacceptable risks to workers, neighbours and the general public.

10. The hours of working on the construction of the development, and deliveries to/collection from the development site shall only take place between the hours of 7.30am and 6.00pm on Monday to Friday; 8.00am and 1.00pm on Saturday with no working taking place on Sundays, Bank and Public Holidays.

Reason
In the interests of residential amenity.

POSITIVE AND PROACTIVE STATEMENT

There were no problems for which the Local Planning Authority had to seek a solution in relation to this application.

NOTES TO APPLICANT

1. Pursuant to Sections 149 and 151 of the Highways Act 1980, steps shall be taken to ensure that mud or other extraneous material is not carried out of the site and deposited on the public highway. Should such deposits occur, it is the applicant's responsibility to ensure that all reasonable steps (e.g. street sweeping) are taken to maintain the roads in the vicinity of the site to a satisfactory level of cleanliness.

2. Due to the location of the site within a residential area the applicant should take all reasonably practicable steps to minimise noise and dust nuisance that may arise from activities on site. The applicant is also advised that material arising from the clearance of vegetation should not be burnt on site in order to prevent smoke nuisance being caused to neighbouring properties.

Officer: Steven Burgoyne
Signed:
Date: 14/08/2015

Checked By:
Date: 14/8/15

The Completed House

End of a long but rewarding journey!

www.straightforwardbooks.co.uk

All titles, listed below, in the Straightforward Guides Series, and further books in the Emerald Guides Series, can be purchased online (Via Amazon) by going to:

www.straightfowardbooks.co.uk

Law, Including Emerald Guides

Consumer Rights
Bankruptcy Insolvency and the Law
Employment Law
Healthcare Rights and law
Negligence in Healthcare
Private Tenants Rights
Family law
Small Claims in the County Court
Contract law
Intellectual Property and the law
Divorce and the law
Leaseholders Rights
The Process of Conveyancing
Knowing Your Rights and Using the Courts
Producing your own Will
Housing Rights

The Bailiff the law and You
Probate and The Law
Company law
What to Expect When You Go to Court
Give me Your Money-Guide to Effective Debt Collection
Being a Litigant in Person
Conveyancing Residential property
A Practical Guide to Obtaining Probate
Marriage and Same Sex Partnerships
A Guide to Powers of Attorney
Mental Health and the Law

General titles, Including Emerald Guides

Letting Property for Profit
Buying, Selling and Renting property
Bookkeeping and Accounts for Small Business
Creative Writing
Freelance Writing
Writing Your own Life Story
Writing performance Poetry
Writing Romantic Fiction
Speech Writing
The Straightforward Business Plan
The Straightforward C.V.
Successful Public Speaking

Handling Bereavement

Individual and Personal Finance

The Crime Writers casebook

Being a Detective

A Comprehensive Guide to Arrest and Detention

A Comprehensive Guide to Burglary and Robbery

The Bailiff and You

Beating The Bully

Explaining Autism

Explaining Diabetes

Explaining Alzheimer's and Dementia

Explaining Asthma

Stop Smoking Now

Mind Power and Healthy Eating

Go to:

www.straightforwardbooks.co.uk

The Planning System and Planning Permissions in the UK

FURTHER BOOKS IN THE PLANNING SERIES

A STRAIGHTFORWARD GUIDE TO DESIGNING AND BUILDING YOUR OWN HOME

ROGER SPROSTON WITH PAUL AND JAYNE MARSHALL

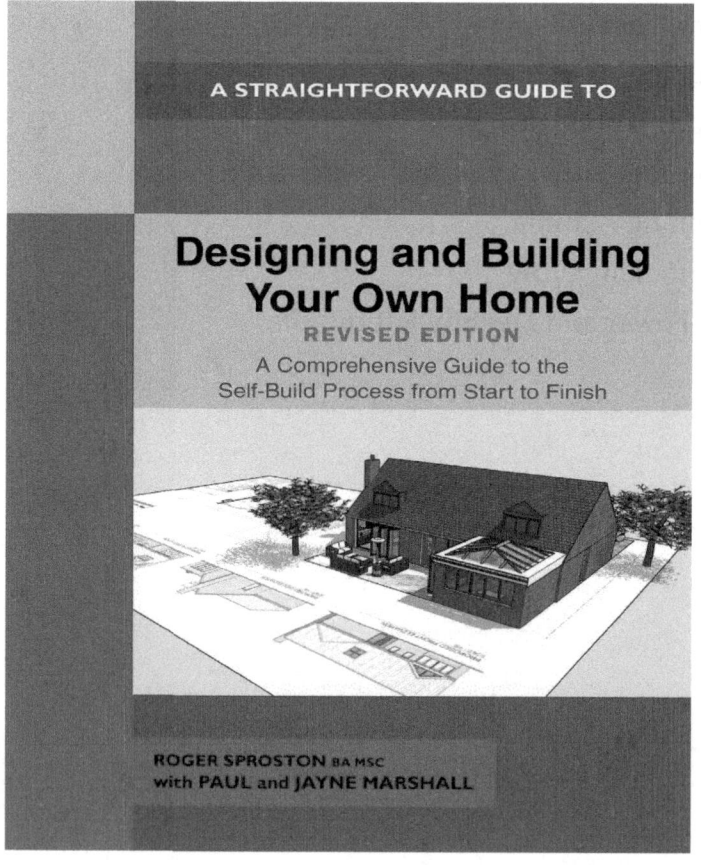

ISBN: 978-1-80236-351-7 £11.99